Jerry S. Kelly

Social Choice Theory

An Introduction

With 77 Figures

Springer-Verlag Berlin Heidelberg GmbH

Prof. Jerry S. Kelly
Syracuse University
Department of Economics
Maxwell Hall
Syracuse, New York 13210
USA

ISBN 978-3-662-09927-8   ISBN 978-3-662-09925-4 (eBook)
DOI 10.1007/978-3-662-09925-4

Library of Congress Cataloging in Publication Data
Kelly, Jerry S. Social choice theory.
1. Social choice. I. Title.
HB846.8.K44   1987   302′.13   87-12858

© Springer-Verlag Berlin Heidelberg 1988
Originally published by Springer-Verlag Berlin Heidelberg New York in 1988
Softcover reprint of the hardcover 1st edition 1988

2142/3140-543210

For Courtney

Table of Contents

Guide to Chapter Dependencies

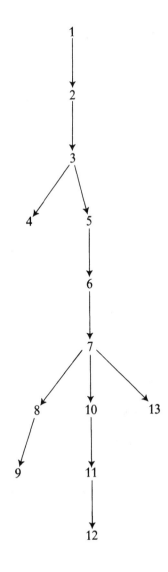

To the Student

What does this text assume you bring as preparation? Actually very little in terms of prior course work:

1. A level of mathematical maturity equal to a good high school algebra sequence. The emphasis is on the level of maturity; relatively little specific detail from algebra will be used.

2. Comfort with set theory ideas and operations, although what is needed is presented in the Mathematical Appendix, which you may wish to examine first. Important also is the ability to recognize and follow rigorous proofs and, soon, to be able to create proofs of your own.

3. Helpful, but certainly not necessary, would be some familiarity with the economist's consumer model of rational behavior based on preference orderings.

4. If you have encountered some political philosophy in a more classical style, whether as ancient as Plato's *Republic* or as recent as Rawls' *Theory of Justice,* you will better appreciate the magnitude of the shift in the social choice approach (see the Introduction).

But beyond these specifics, what is most required is an appreciation of the value of abstracting out the essence of an idea from a lot of distracting surrounding detail (in the manner of the economist's model of a consumer). While we will be very concerned with ways of making social choices, you will not find anything here about the interplay of personalities and political institutions or about the historical matrix within which that interplay occurs. That is, of course, a great loss, but it allows us to focus with special clarity on social choice rules and the criteria we wish them to satisfy.

One final word about reading this text. If you don't understand a word, a sentence or an example, read on for a few pages; sometimes later material will help clarify what comes just before. But if you still don't understand something, seek your instructor's help before proceeding too far. This material is very cumulative and an early misunderstanding can quickly snowball into much confusion. Getting it right early can be rewarding.

Acknowledgements

I owe many thanks to all the students I have had in several social choice courses at Syracuse University; they have helped tremendously, making me rethink and reexplain social choice ideas and have helped me see the centrality of exercises in learning these ideas. For reading earlier drafts of this material and providing many useful comments I am indebted to Fred Frohock, Stuart Thorson, Wulf Gaertner and, above all, to Bruce Riddle.

Chapter 0. What is Social Choice Theory?

O.K., What is social choice theory?

Social Choice Theory is the study of systems and institutions for making collective choices, choices that affect a group of people.

Why study social choice theory?

For one thing, social choice theory has a very practical side in aiding selection of a procedure for making choices by political or social organizations. This kind of choice is illustrated by the recent discussion by French President Francoise Mitterand's Socialist Party to change the method for selecting deputies to Parliament. The two-stage winner-take-all system instituted by de Gaulle's Fifth Republic will be replaced by a single vote proportional system.[1] Social choice theorists have intensively studied these systems.[2] It also has a semi-practical side in providing a framework within which discussions about evaluating social choices can be formulated (social choice theory had its origin in theoretical welfare economics where this side was the goal)[3]. But its potentially most important side is in allowing us to make real progress in answering some of the oldest questions in political philosophy[4]. While philosophy doesn't have a reputation for progress, for building new questions on successful answers to old questions, there is a history of disciplines breaking away from philosophy to do just this. Psychology broke off to provide progress on questions of mind; logic broke off to provide progress on questions of reasoning and evidence. Social choice theory is breaking off to provide progress on political philosophy questions about how societies ought to be making collective choices.

---

[1] Bernstein, Richard, "France Adopting New Voting Plan," *New York Times* (April 4, 1985), p. A7.

[2] See, for example, Douglas Rae's *Political Consequences of Electoral Laws* (Yale, 1971); *Choosing an Electoral System* edited by Arend Lijphart and Bernard Grofman (N.Y.: Praeger, 1984); and Vernon Bogdanor's *Democracy and Elections: Electoral Systems and Their Political Consequences* (Cambridge University Press, 1984). Michael Dummett's *Voting Procedures* (Oxford University Press, 1984) builds bridges from this more practical literature to the social choice theory developed in this text.

[3] See, for example, Allan Feldman's *Welfare Economics and Social Choice Theory* (Martinus Nijhoff, 1980).

[4] See William Riker's *Liberalism Against Populism* (Freeman, 1982).

These are not just peripheral questions; they are near the heart of our concept of what we are:[5]

For the Greeks, a cardinal human quality was the ability to establish the political and social order embodied in the city-state; men at their best could set collective goals, make laws and obey them, and none of these could be achieved by animals in a state of nature.

Do you mean to say social choice theorists have finally answered the classical questions of political philosophers?

No, that's not the point. I mean they have developed a *cumulative* enterprise that is chipping away at the edge of political philosophy, finding out which questions *have* what kinds of answers. When philosophers asked: What is life? and confronted that question head-on, little progress was made. What we understand today about answering that question is built from the cumulative research on little details by molecular biologists. When philosophers asked: What is the origin of the universe? and confronted that question head-on, little progress was made. What we now see as an answer to that question is built from cumulative research on details, in this case by radio astronomers and particle physicists. So instead of confronting head-on a question like: What rights ought people have? we might do better by working in a cumulative way on details like what assignments of rights are *possible* (see Chapter 9). This is the kind of thing social choice theorists do.

But don't we know the best answer to the main social choice question anyway? Collective decisions ought to be made democratically through majority voting.

First, democracy is *not* the same as the particular implementing procedure of majority voting. There are many social choice procedures we might consider "democratic."

Second, which of those procedures we should use, or even whether we might sometimes adopt a non-"democratic" procedure depends on what evaluative criteria we adopt. We will spend a lot of space in this book being very careful about defining criteria and exploring what they mean. Along these lines, we might as well announce now that some of the most important results in social choice theory are *impossibility theorems*. These are rigorously obtained results showing that, given a list of criteria that we would like a social choice procedure to satisfy, it isn't possible for *any* social choice rule to satisfy all of them.

---

[5] Bolter, J. David, *Turing's Man* (University of North Carolina Press, 1984) p. 9.

But if none work, social choice theory doesn't give us reasons for choosing something other than majority voting.

That *doesn't* follow. In fact, along the way we will have nice things to say about procedures with names like *Borda rule* and *approval voting.* But to help you break away from a naive advocacy of majority voting we will begin this book with several chapters providing a close examination of that procedure and its problems.

I've leafed through the book and there seem to be lots of exercises.

There are a bit more than 250 exercises, and they are the heart of the book. Social choice criteria are often quite slippery and subtle; experience shows that you are unlikely to understand them unless you get your hands dirty working on the exercises. Don't read this book without doing the exercises.

Chapter 1. Simple Majority Voting

Suppose as a group we must choose one of two possible outcomes. It might be a choice of President from candidates of two parties or a decision about whether or not to permit the humpback whale to become extinct. It might be a decision about building or not building an anti-ballistic missile system or conviction versus acquittal. For the moment we don't care about any special details about these two possible outcomes so we will give them very neutral names. For brevity we might choose 'yea' and 'nay', but we go one step further. One is called 'x' and the other is called 'y'.

The next thing we are going to do is go out and collect information to help make the choice between these. What information should we gather? We might go after more details about these alternatives; we might determine what some religious tract or oracle tells us; we might observe the outcome of a coin toss. But we aren't going to do any of those things. Let's simplify our problem a bit by assuming that everybody already knows enough details about the alternatives that we don't have to seek out more. As for religious tracts, they have little to say on Lincoln vs. Douglas, deterrence vs. defense or about what species to preserve. Modern oracles might have more to say about these, but few of us would trust our political judgements to them. Coin tosses may be helpful at the *end* of our procedures if they get stalemated, but there are good things we might try before resorting to that.

A classic "democratic" answer to our question is that we ought to go out and gather from the individuals concerned their considered judgements about the two alternatives. This already gives us enormously complicated issues to deal with:

A.) Whose judgement should be considered? Everyone in the group? No matter how young? or irresponsible? No matter how unaffected by the outcome? How, for that matter, do we decide who is in a group? How do we set the rules for club membership? How do we formulate laws determining citizenship?
B.) How can we hope to get judgements that are "considered" and thoughtful, that really are considered judgements and not just whims or bizarre prejudices?
C.) How can we be sure that people will correctly and honestly reveal their judgements?

We are going to simply ignore the first question and assume that a set N of voters, n in number, has been selected. As for the second question, we are not going to consider paternalistically evaluating judgements to determine which are good enough to be incorporated (at least we won't consider that until Chapter 9). From each of the n voters we accept a decision that i) x is strictly better than y or ii) y is strictly better than x or iii) that x and y are equivalent, i.e., that the voter is indifferent between x and y.

This is the *only* information collected. If you are a voter, you can record your preference for x over y but not that you like x "twice as much as" y or that you would pay $100 to get x instead of y or that if y wins you will emigrate. You can not append to your ballot a list of six reasons behind your preference or an affidavit that you have spent four years of scholarly study scrutinizing the policy issues concerning x and y.

Since the information is so simple, it can be easily coded. We will let $+1$ stand for a preference for x over y; -1 stand for y over x and 0 stand for indifference. So from each voter we collect $+1$, -1 or 0. Since there are n voters, we will have n coded preferences, n numbers. If we imagine our voters lined up in some order (maybe by height or alphabetically) we can see the information gathered as an ordered list of $+1$'s, -1's and 0's. If everyone without exception preferred x to y we would collect a list like

$$\underbrace{(+1, +1, +1, ..., +1, +1).}_{\text{n entries}}$$

But preferences might be more varied and we might collect a mixed list

$$(+1, -1, +1, ..., 0, -1).$$

In this informational context, a social choice rule will be a function (see the Mathematical Appendix) or mapping that associates with lists of this sort the corresponding outcome: x wins or y wins or x and y tie. These outcomes are also simple enough to code easily. We will use $+1$ to indicate that x wins; -1 to represent y winning and 0 to display a tie. So a social choice rule is a mapping that associates with lists of $+1$, -1 and 0 the resulting outcome numbers $+1$, -1 or 0. To illustrate the idea we point out three extreme social choice rules, called the constant functions (see the Mathematical Appendix): const_{+1} associates with all possible lists the same outcome, $+1$; const_{-1} associates with all possible lists the same outcome, -1; const_0 associates with all possible lists the same outcome, 0. Each of these rules effectively ignores all the information gathered in the list since each gives an outcome that never varies as the list varies. Const_0 also doesn't help in choosing since it never narrows down the choice; it always shows x and y tied.

The rule we here call *simple majority voting* can be defined as soon as we introduce a few pieces of notation. The first is for a general list or list variable. A general list will be written

$$D = (d_1, d_2, d_3, ..., d_{n-1}, d_n)$$

where each d_i is $+1$, -1, or 0 depending on whether individual i strictly prefers x to y, y to x or is indifferent between them. In simple majority voting we focus, at list $(d_1, d_2, d_3, ..., d_{n-1}, d_n)$, on the sum

$$d_1 + d_2 + d_3 + ... + d_{n-1} + d_n.$$

If this sum is positive, then each different -1 term in the sum is offset by a different

+1 term and there is at least one +1 term left over. That is, every individual who prefers y to x can be paired with someone who prefers x to y and after the pairing is over there remain unpaired people who prefer x to y. We are simply saying that more people prefer x to y than prefer y to x and simple majority voting should then say x is to be chosen. So:

$$\text{When } d_1 + d_2 + d_3 + \ldots + d_{n-1} + d_n > 0,$$
$$\text{simple majority voting assigns } +1.$$

Correspondingly, when this sum is negative, more people prefer y to x than prefer x to y and so simple majority voting should then say y is to be chosen. So:

$$\text{When } d_1 + d_2 + d_3 + \ldots + d_{n-1} + d_n < 0,$$
$$\text{simple majority voting assigns } -1.$$

Finally, if this sum is zero, we can pair each individual who prefers x to y with an individual who prefers y to x; when this pairing is completed, the only people left over are indifferent between x and y; x and y have tied. So:

$$\text{When } d_1 + d_2 + d_3 + \ldots + d_{n-1} + d_n = 0,$$
$$\text{simple majority voting assigns } 0.$$

To express these rules more succinctly, we use a standard mathematical function, the sign function, sgn. When the sign function looks at a number x it assigns +1, −1 or 0 according as x is positive, negative or zero; for example,

$$\text{sgn} -3 = -1; \text{sgn} +7 = \text{sgn} \sqrt{2} = +1; \text{sgn} 0 = 0.$$

Then *simple majority vote* is formally defined by the assignment

$$(d_1, d_2, \ldots, d_n) \rightarrow \text{sgn} (d_1 + d_2 + \ldots + d_n).$$

Now before we talk about the properties of this rule, it is important to be clear about the distinction between this rule and one that is closely related. First define a function N_{+1} that associates with a list $(d_1, d_2, \ldots, d_n)$ the number of d_i's that are strictly positive and also define a function N_{-1} that associates with that list the number of d_i's that are strictly negative:

$$N_{+1}(+1, -1, 0, 0, +1, -1, +1) = 3;$$
$$N_{-1}(+1, -1, 0, 0, +1, -1, +1) = 2.$$

Using these two functions, we could have defined simple majority voting by assigning the value +1 if $N_{+1}(d_1, d_2, \ldots, d_n)$ is greater than $N_{-1}(d_1, d_2, \ldots, d_n)$; −1 if less and 0 if equal. That is, simple majority voting assigns +1 if $N_{+1}(d_1, d_2, \ldots, d_n)$ is greater than half of the number of individuals who aren't indifferent between x and y. All this is by way of contrast with a new rule that compares $N_{+1}(d_1, d_2, \ldots, d_n)$ with half the number of all individuals rather than with half the number of individuals who aren't indifferent between x and y.

$$g(d_1, d_2, \ldots, d_n) = \begin{cases} +1 \text{ if } N_{+1}(d_1, d_2, \ldots, d_n) > n/2 \\ -1 \text{ if } N_{-1}(d_1, d_2, \ldots, d_n) > n/2 \\ 0 \text{ otherwise} \end{cases}$$

Faced with the list $(+1, +1, +1, 0, 0, -1, -1)$, this new rule would assign 0 since neither the number of positive entries in the list nor the number of negative entries exceeds 7/2. On the other hand, simple majority voting faced with this list would assign +1 since the positive entries outnumber negative. Let's call the new rule *absolute majority voting*.

Exercises.
1. Show that for simple majority voting to yield 0 when the number of individuals is odd, a necessary condition is that at least one individual must be indifferent between x and y.
2. Show that this condition of Exercise 1 is not sufficient for simple majority voting to yield zero when the number of individuals is odd.
3. Show that if simple majority voting gives 0 so does absolute majority voting.
4. Show that with simple majority voting and absolute majority voting one can't give +1 when the other gives −1.

We now seek a list of properties of simple majority voting. In particular, we seek a set of *characteristic properties*. By this we mean a set of properties such that a rule satisfies all of them if and only if it is simple majority voting. This was first done by the late mathematician and historian of mathematics Kenneth O. May in 1952. It is toward May's result that we now develop this chapter. We will let a social choice rule be indicated by the letter f and the outcome of the rule at $(d_1, d_2, ..., d_n)$ will be written $f(d_1, d_2, ..., d_n)$. The *domain* (see the Mathematical Appendix) of a rule is the set of all lists to which f assigns some unambiguous outcome: +1, −1 or 0. We are not interested in rules that don't clearly and unambiguously assign a value. Imagine a "rule" that says $f(+1, +1, +1, 0, 0, -1, -1)$ is 0 if there is a manned expedition to Mars during the year 2090; otherwise +1 is assigned. Such a "rule" does not *now* give a well-defined result and so is not now very useful. Of course, by 2091, this rule would be well-defined at this list.

Simple majority voting is in this sense defined over a large domain, the largest possible; that is, simple majority voting satisfies the property of *universal domain* :

f satisfies universal domain if it has a
domain equal to all logically possible lists of
n entries of +1, −1 or 0.

The second property (of four) we consider is *anonymity*[1]. A social choice rule will satisfy this property if it doesn't make any difference *who* votes in which way as long as the numbers of each type are the same. For example the lists

$$(+1, +1, +1, 0, 0, -1, -1)$$

and

$$(-1, 0, +1, +1, 0, -1, +1)$$

---

[1] The reader should be warned about the use here, as technical terms, of words that have a different meaning in natural language. Anonymity here means something like equal treatment rather than something like secret ballots.

Exercises.

5. Observe that universal domain is satisfied not only by simple majority voting but also by absolute majority voting and by the constant rule const_0.
6. Determine if universal domain is satisfied by the rule

$$f(d_1, \ldots, d_n) = \begin{cases} +1 \text{ if } N_{+1}(d_1, \ldots, d_n) > n/2 \\ -1 \text{ if } N_{-1}(d_1, \ldots, d_n) > n/2 \\ 0 \text{ if } N_{+1}(d_1, \ldots, d_n) = n/2 \\ \quad \text{and} \\ \quad N_{-1}(d_1, \ldots, d_n) = n/2. \end{cases}$$

7. Determine if universal domain is satisfied by the rule

$$f(d_1, \ldots, d_n) = \text{sgn } N_{+1}(d_1, \ldots, d_n).$$

are simple rearrangements of one another; exactly who has the $+1$ votes though is different in the two lists. The lists are said to be "permutations" of each other. If f satisfies anonymity and these two lists are both in the domain, then if $+1$ is assigned to the first it is also assigned to the second. Anonymous social choice rules assign the same value to any two lists in the domain that are permutations of one another.

To give all this some precision, we introduce the idea of a *one-to-one correspondence.* A one-to-one correspondence on the set $\{1, 2, \ldots, n\}$ is a function s from this set to itself such that s is defined on every integer from 1 to n (so the domain of s is all of the set) and no outcome is assigned to two different integers:

$$s(i) = s(j) \text{ implies } i = j.$$

The function s given by

$$1 \rightarrow 1, 2 \rightarrow 3, 3 \rightarrow 4, 4 \rightarrow 2$$

is one-to-one on $\{1, 2, 3, 4\}$ but

$$1 \rightarrow 1, 2 \rightarrow 3, 3 \rightarrow 4, 4 \rightarrow 3$$

is not because 3 is assigned to both 2 and 4.

Exercise.

8. Show that if s is a one-to-one correspondence on $\{1, 2, \ldots, n\}$, then for every $k, 1 \leq k \leq n$, there is an i with $k = s(i)$.

Given two lists

$$(d_1, d_2, \ldots, d_n)$$

and

$$(d_1', d_2', \ldots, d_n')$$

we say that they are *permutations* of one another if there is a one-to-one correspondence s on $\{1, 2, \ldots, n\}$ such that

$$d_{s(i)}' = d_i.$$

Thus

$$(+1, +1, +1, 0, 0, -1, -1)$$

and

$$(-1, 0, +1, +1, 0, -1, +1)$$

are permutations of one another via the one-to-one correspondence

$$1\rightarrow3, 2\rightarrow4, 3\rightarrow7,$$
$$4\rightarrow2, 5\rightarrow5, 6\rightarrow1,$$
$$7\rightarrow6.$$

Finally a social choice rule f satisfies *anonymity* if whenever $(d_1, d_2, ..., d_n)$ and $(d_1', d_2', ..., d_n')$ in the domain of f are permutations of one another then

$$f(d_1, d_2, ..., d_n) = f(d_1', d_2', ..., d_n').$$

Exercises.

9. Show that d and itself are permutations of one another.
10. If d and d' are permutations of one another, then d' and d are permutations of one another. (Exercises expressed as declarative sentences are requests for you to prove what is stated.)
11. If d and d' are permutations of one another and d' and d" are permutations of one another, then d and d" are permutations of one another.
12. Show that simple majority voting, absolute majority voting and the three constant rules all satisfy anonymity.
13. Determine if anonymity is satisfied by the rule of Exercise 7:

$$f(d_1, d_2, ..., d_n) = \text{sgn } N_{+1}(d_1, ..., d_n).$$

14. Determine if anonymity is satisfied by the rule
$$f(d_1, d_2, ..., d_n) = d_1.$$

While the condition of anonymity is a way of treating individuals equally, the next condition is a way of treating alternatives x and y equally. A social choice rule satisfies *neutrality* if whenever $(d_1, d_2, ..., d_n)$ and $(-d_1, -d_2, ..., -d_n)$ are both in the domain of f then

$$f(-d_1, -d_2, ..., -d_n) = -f(d_1, d_2, ..., d_n).$$

A social choice rule satisfies neutrality if, whenever everyone reverses their preference between x and y, then the result is reversed (and if there was a tie, there still is). For example, the constant rule const_{+1} fails neutrality because both $f(d_1, d_2, ..., d_n)$ and $f(-d_1, -d_2, ..., -d_n)$ are $+1$ while neutrality requires that $f(d_1, d_2, ..., d_n) = +1$ implies $f(-d_1, -d_2, ..., -d_n) = -1$. A neutral rule could not have both $f(+1, 0, -1, +1, 0) = +1$ and $f(-1, 0, +1, -1, 0) = 0$.

The three conditions (universal domain, anonymity and neutrality) we have detailed so far are still consistent with very perverse rules. For example, Exercises 5, 12 and 15 show that all three conditions are satisfied by the rule const_0 that assigns 0 to every list. Such a rule is very unresponsive to the preferences of the members of the

Exercises.

15. Show that simple majority voting, absolute majority voting and the constant rule const_0 all satisfy neutrality.

16. Determine if neutrality is satisfied by the rule of Exercise 7:

$$f(d_1, \ldots, d_n) = \text{sgn } N_{+1}(d_1, \ldots, d_n).$$

17. Determine if neutrality is satisfied by the rule of Exercise 14:

$$f(d_1, \ldots, d_n) = d_1.$$

group and so our fourth and last condition is designed to introduce some responsiveness. To describe this responsiveness condition, we first define a new concept that in different guises will prove useful throughout this book. Suppose

$$D = (d_1, d_2, \ldots, d_n)$$

and

$$D' = (d_1', d_2', \ldots, d_n')$$

are two lists; we say D and D' are *i-variants* if for all $j \neq i$, $d_j = d_j'$. Thus two i-variants differ in at most the *i*th entry. So, for example,

$$(+1, +1, +1, 0, 0, -1, -1)$$

and

$$(+1, +1, +1, 0, 0, 0, -1)$$

are 6-variants since they differ only at the sixth place.

Exercises.

18. When can D and D' be both 1-variants and 2-variants? [Hint: The answer is *not* "never."]

19. Show that if D and D' are i-variants and also D' and D'' are i-variants, then D and D'' are i-variants.

Now suppose $(d_1, d_2, \ldots, d_n)$ and $(d_1', d_2', \ldots, d_n')$ are i-variants and that $d_i' > d_i$. This means that, for individual i, x has improved relative to y; either y was preferred to x and now x is preferred to or indifferent with y or x and y were indifferent and now x is preferred to y. If $f(d_1, \ldots, d_n) = +1$, i.e., x won and now the only change is that x has risen in i's order we would want x still to win. If $f(d_1, \ldots, d_n) = 0$, then we would want $f(d_1, \ldots, d_n) \geq 0$, i.e., if x and y were tied and x rose in i's order we don't want y now to win. All this is still not enough, though, because the constant rule, const_0, satisfies all these conditions. So we modify this a little bit by insisting that if x and y were tied and now x rises in i's order then this is enough to break the tie in x's favor.

Definition. f satisfies *positive responsiveness* if for all i, whenever $(d_1, d_2, \ldots, d_n)$ and $(d_1', d_2', \ldots, d_n')$ are i-variants with $d_i' > d_i$, then

$$f(d_1, \ldots, d_n) \geq 0 \text{ implies } f(d_1', \ldots, d_n') = +1.$$

Exercises.
20. Show that simple majority voting satisfies positive responsiveness.
21. Show that the $const_1$ and $const_{-1}$ rules satisfy positive responsiveness. (That shows you how imperfect the terminology is; these rules are as unresponsive as possible.)
22. Show absolute majority rule and the $const_0$ rules do *not* satisfy positive responsiveness.
23. Determine if positive responsiveness is satisfied by the rule of Exercise 7:

$$f(d_1, \ldots, d_n) = \operatorname{sgn} N_{+1}(d_1, \ldots, d_n).$$

24. Determine if positive responsiveness is satisfied by the rule of Exercise 14:

$$f(d_1, \ldots, d_n) = d_1.$$

There are three remarks to be made about this positive responsiveness condition.

Remark 1. We might sometimes want to make successive applications of the condition. If f satisfies positive responsiveness and

$$f(+1, 0, -1, 0, 0, +1, -1) = 0$$

then

$$f(+1, 0, 0, +1, 0, +1, -1) = +1.$$

There is no i such that these two lists are i-variants since they differ at two places. But $(+1, 0, 0, 0, 0, +1, -1)$ is a 3-variant of the first and a 4-variant of the second. From

$$f(+1, 0, -1, 0, 0, +1, -1) = 0$$

and positive responsiveness we get

$$f(+1, 0, 0, 0, 0, +1, -1) = +1;$$

then a second application of positive responsiveness yields

$$f(+1, 0, 0, +1, 0, +1, -1) = +1.$$

Exercise.
25. Suppose f satisfies universal domain and positive responsiveness and that f is *not* $const_{-1}$. Does this ensure

$$f(+1, +1, \ldots, +1) = +1?$$

Remark 2. There is a strange asymmetry built into our definition of positive responsiveness. The condition details the consequences of a rise of x relative to y in someone's order but doesn't insist upon responsiveness to a rise of y relative to x. But we are going to consider positive responsiveness simultaneously with neutrality and in this context we also get responsiveness with respect to a rise in y. To illustrate this, suppose f yields 0 (i.e., a tie) at list D defined by

$$D = (0, +1, -1, 0, 0, +1, -1).$$

Now suppose y rises relative to x for individual #2 in moving to a 2-variant list D' defined by

$$D' = (0, 0, -1, 0, 0, +1, -1) \qquad .$$

We want to show that at this new list f yields -1 (i.e., y wins). To see this, consider the list

$$-D = (0, -1, +1, 0, 0, -1, +1).$$

By neutrality, $f(-D) = -f(D) = -0 = 0$. Now, from $-D$ advance x relative to y in #2's order to get 2-variant list

$$D^* = (0, 0, +1, 0, 0, -1, +1).$$

Positive responsiveness tells us that $f(D^*) = +1$. Since $D^* = -D'$, a second application of neutrality then shows $f(D') = -f(-D') = -f(D^*) = -1$ which is what we wanted.

Exercise.

26. If f satisfies universal domain, positive responsiveness and neutrality, then

$$f(+1, +1, \ldots, +1) = +1$$

and

$$f(-1, -1, \ldots, -1) = -1.$$

Remark 3. All four conditions are satisfied by simple majority voting. This is seen by Exercises 5, 12, 15 and 20. It is the central idea of the next theorem that simple majority voting is the *only* rule that satisfies all four simultaneously. This theorem ensures then, that these are characterizing properties of the sort we had hoped to find.

Theorem (May[2]). If a social choice rule f satisfies all of

  i) universal domain;
  ii) anonymity;
  iii) neutrality;
  iv) positive responsiveness;

then f is simple majority voting.

Proof. The proof is structured into three steps. In Step 1, it is shown that if f satisfies all four conditions, then $f(D)$ at list D will depend only on $N_{+1}(D)$ and $N_{-1}(D)$. In Step 2 it is shown that we must have $f(D) = 0$ if $N_{+1}(D) = N_{-1}(D)$, i.e., f must coincide with simple majority voting on those lists with equal numbers of $+1$s and -1s. Finally Step 3 extends the coincidence of f and simple majority voting to all other lists.

Step 1. We first observe that because f satisfies anonymity the value of $f(d_1, \ldots, d_n)$ doesn't depend on the *positions* of the $+1$'s, -1's and 0's in the list and so only depends on the *numbers* of $+1$'s, -1's and 0's. Given n, the number of $+1$'s, $N_{+1}(d_1, ..., d_n)$, and the number of -1's, $N_{-1}(d_1, ..., d_n)$, we can get the number of 0's as

$$n - N_{+1}(d_1, d_2, ..., d_n) - N_{-1}(d_1, d_2, ..., d_n);$$

the number of 0's is not an independent piece of information. So anonymity implies that $f(d_1, d_2, ..., d_n)$ is entirely determined by $N_{+1}(d_1, d_2, ..., d_n)$ and $N_{-1}(d_1, d_2, ..., d_n)$.

Step 2. Suppose $N_{+1}(d_1, d_2, ..., d_n) = N_{-1}(d_1, d_2, ..., d_n)$ and $f(d_1, d_2, ..., d_n)$ takes the value d. Look at the situation $(-d_1, -d_2, ..., -d_n)$. By universal domain, f is defined at this new situation. Since

$$N_{+1}(-d_1, -d_2, ..., -d_n) = N_{-1}(d_1, d_2, ..., d_n)$$
$$= N_{+1}(d_1, d_2, ..., d_n)$$

and

$$N_{-1}(-d_1, -d_2, ..., -d_n) = N_{+1}(d_1, d_2, ..., d_n)$$
$$= N_{-1}(d_1, d_2, ..., d_n),$$

we get from Step 1 that $f(-d_1, -d_2, ..., -d_n) = f(d_1, d_2, ..., d_n) = d$. But since f satisfies neutrality, $f(-d_1, -d_2, ..., -d_n) = -d$. Combining these, $d = -d$ so $d = 0$. Summarizing, $N_{+1}(d_1, d_2, ..., d_n) = N_{-1}(d_1, d_2, ..., d_n)$ implies $f(d_1, d_2, ..., d_n) = 0$.

Step 3. Suppose now $N_{+1}(d_1, d_2, ..., d_n) > N_{-1}(d_1, d_2, ..., d_n)$. We wish to show $f(d_1, d_2, ..., d_n)$ then must be $+1$. An analogous derivation (or an appeal to neutrality) would then show that $f(d_1, d_2, ..., d_n) = -1$ when $N_{+1}(d_1, d_2, ..., d_n) < N_{-1}(d_1, d_2, ..., d_n)$. These two results together with the result of Step 2, says f works just like simple majority voting which is what we wish to prove.

So we are supposing $N_{+1}(d_1, d_2, ..., d_n) = N_{-1}(d_1, d_2, ..., d_n) + m$ where m is a positive integer (no larger than $n - N_{-1}(d_1, d_2, ..., d_n)$). We will prove $f(d_1, d_2, ..., d_n) = +1$ by mathematical induction (see the Mathematical Appendix).

Basis step: $m = 1$. Since $N_{+1}(d_1, d_2, ..., d_n) = N_{-1}(d_1, d_2, ..., d_n) + 1$, at least one $d_i = 1$. Examine another situation, $(d_1', d_2', ..., d_n')$, an i-variant determined by

$$d_j' = d_j \text{ if } j \neq i;$$
$$d_i' = 0.$$

f is defined there and at $(d_1, d_2, ..., d_n)$ by universal domain. Clearly $N_{+1}(d_1', d_2', ..., d_n') = N_{-1}(d_1', d_2', ..., d_n')$ and Step 2 tells us $f(d_1', d_2', ..., d_n') = 0$. This together with positive responsiveness yields $f(d_1, d_2, ..., d_n) = +1$.

Induction step: Now suppose $N_{+1}(d_1, d_2, ..., d_n) = N_{-1}(d_1, d_2, ..., d_n) + m$ implies $f(d_1, d_2, ..., d_n) = +1$. We have to show that $N_{+1}(d_1, d_2, ..., d_n) = N_{-1}(d_1, d_2, ..., d_n) + (m+1)$ implies $f(d_1, d_2, ..., d_n) = +1$. So suppose $N_{+1}(d_1, d_2, ..., d_n) = N_{-1}(d_1, d_2, ..., d_n) + (m+1)$. At least one $d_i = +1$. Define an i-variant situation $(d_1', d_2', ..., d_n')$ by

$$d_j' = d_j \text{ if } j \neq i;$$
$$d_i' = 0.$$

Again, f is defined at both $(d_1, d_2, ..., d_n)$ and $(d_1', d_2', ..., d_n')$ and at this second list we clearly have $N_{+1}(d_1', d_2', ..., d_n') = N_{-1}(d_1', d_2', ..., d_n') + m$. The induction hypothesis yields $f(d_1', d_2', ..., d_n') = +1$. Applying positive responsiveness we have $f(d_1, d_2, ..., d_n) = +1$. ∎

Exercises.

27. We have encountered several rules besides simple majority voting: the three constant rules, absolute majority voting, and the rules of Exercises 6, 7 and 14. For each of these tell which conditions of May's theorem are not satisfied.

28. The four conditions of May's theorem are *completely independent.* This means
    a. We can find a rule satisfying all four conditions;
    b. For each condition we can find a rule violating that one while satisfying the other three simultaneously;
    c. For each pair of conditions we can find a rule satisfying that pair while violating the other two;
    d. For each condition, we can find a rule satisfying that condition while violating the other three;
    e. We can find a rule violating all four conditions.
    You should construct 16 rules to confirm this complete independence.

29. Can we similarly characterize absolute majority voting?
    a. Show that absolute majority voting satisfies the condition of *strong nonreversibility:*

    $$\text{If } D' = D \text{ except that } d_i' = 0 \text{ for one i for whom}$$
    $$d_i = 1, \text{ then } f(D) \geq 0 \text{ implies } f(D') \geq 0.$$

    b. Show that absolute majority voting satisfies the following two monotonicity conditions:
    I) If D' is an i-variant of D with $D_i' \geq D_i$, then $f(D') \geq f(D)$.
    II) If at D, no d_i is 0 and D' is obtained from D by changing some $d_i = -1$ to $d_i' = +1$, then $f(D) \geq 0$ implies $f(D') = +1$.

    Peter Fishburn[3] has shown that absolute majority voting is completely characterized by these three conditions together with universal domain, anonymity and neutrality.

---

[3] Fishburn, Peter, *The Theory of Social Choice* (Princeton University Press, 1973).

Chapter 2. The Voting Paradox

We now have a fairly clear sense of exactly what simple majority voting is and what a set of characteristic properties for that rule looks like. It is *extremely* important for you to see that simple majority voting has only been defined for the case of exactly two alternatives. Most of the problems with simple majority voting arise in a context of more than two alternatives and all interesting contexts have more than two alternatives. Sometimes this is disguised as when we are asked to make a final choice between two party-selected candidates. But the social choice process for filling office starts with many potential candidates and includes many preliminary narrowing procedures: decisions to run or not run, nominating petitions, primaries, withdrawals, conventions, ... So let's explore what happens when we increase the number of alternatives to three or more, labeled x, y, z ....

One central idea to keep in mind is that there is *not* a *unique* way of extending simple majority voting to make decisions among three or more alternatives. We will illuminate this point now by indicating two very different ways of basing a choice among x, y and z on majority voting. One of these ways will be explored in this and the next two chapters; the other will be taken up again in Chapter 5 where yet more rules based on majority voting will appear. For the first version, we look at the set we are going to choose from and consider *all possible* pairs of distinct alternatives. From the set {x, y, z} these pairs are

$$\{x, y\}, \{x, z\} \text{ and } \{y, z\}.$$

Then simple majority voting is applied to each pair. An alternative is called a *Condorcet winner*[1] if it wins or at least ties in every single vote comparison in which it occurs. For example, suppose x and y tie in simple majority voting applied to {x, y} while x beats z and y also beats z. Then both x and y are Condorcet winners. The first technique for extending simple majority voting, then, is to select from the set of all alternatives just those alternatives that are Condorcet winners.

The second method of extending simple majority voting does *not* make all possible pairwise comparisons. We start with some given ordering of the alternatives called the *managing ordering*; then a sequence of simple majority voting stages occurs. In the first stage, simple majority voting is used to compare the first two al-

---

[1] After Marie Jean Antoine Nicolas Caritat, Marquis de Condorcet, who wrote one of the first significant works on social choice in Paris in 1785: *Essai sur l'Application de l'Analyse la Probabilité des Décisions Rendues la Pluralité des Voix.*

ternatives in the managing ordering and at the second stage the winner of the first stage is pitted in a simple majority voting comparison with the third alternative in the managing ordering. At the third stage, the winner at the second stage is pitted against the fourth alternative and so on. Now this staging procedure only makes sense if at each stage "*the* winner" makes sense: since simple majority voting allows ties, we need to supplement simple majority voting at each stage with a tie-breaking procedure. For example, we might agree that at each stage, if a tie occurs under simple majority voting then the winner will be the alternative that comes first in the managing ordering.

These two methods, the Condorcet winner procedure and the staging extension, are different. For the same pattern of voters' preferences, the two rules may lead to different alternatives being chosen. In this chapter and in Chapters 3 and 4 we will show problems with the Condorcet winner extension; in Chapter 5 we will show problems with the staging extension.

The central difficulty with the Condorcet winner extension of simple majority voting is that sometimes it doesn't even work; sometimes there is no Condorcet winner. Suppose in the simple majority vote comparison on $\{x, y\}$ x alone wins while on $\{y, z\}$ y alone wins and on $\{x, z\}$ z alone wins. Then there is no alternative that comes out beating or tieing every other alternative: x loses to z which loses to y which loses to x. The occurrence of failure of existence of a Condorcet winner is called a *voting paradox*.

How might a voting paradox arise? One possibility occurs in a simple problem of trying to apportion some single highly divisible commodity among several individuals. Suppose there are three individuals who have to divide up a pie that can be split up into any three fractions adding to 1. An *alternative*, then, is a triple, (F_1, F_2, F_3) where F_i is the fraction of the pie going to individual i. We assume each $F_i \geq 0$ and $F_1 + F_2 + F_3 = 1$. Assume also that each individual selfishly votes for one triple over another if and only if the one gives him a larger fraction than the other. For this situation, there is no Condorcet winner. Every alternative loses to some other. For example,

$(0, 0, 1)$ loses to $(1/2, 1/2, 0)$ on votes by individuals #1 and #2;

$(1/2, 1/2, 0)$ loses to $(0, 3/4, 1/4)$ by individuals #2 and #3;

$(0, 3/4, 1/4)$ loses to $(1/3, 0, 2/3)$ by individuals #1 and #3;

$(1/3, 0, 2/3)$ loses to $(9/10, 1/10, 0)$ by individuals #1 and #2;

and so on and on.

More generally, since $F_1 + F_2 + F_3 = 1$, at least one F_i is strictly positive; say $F_1 > 0$. Then (F_1, F_2, F_3) loses to $(0, F_2 + (1/2)F_1, F_3 + (1/2)F_1)$ with #2 and #3 making up a majority. Similar majority vote losses occur if it is F_2 or F_3, known to be positive. The Condorcet winner extension is not a good way for many people to try to allocate a resource fixed in total amount.

Exercise.

30. Generalize this argument to any number of individuals greater than two.
31. Generalize this argument to the case where the components of an alternative add to any positive constant M.
32. Show that the argument does *not* work with two individuals by showing the existence of (many) Condorcet winners then.

Now this example seems to use a huge number of possible alternatives, of possible triples. Can we explain how a voting paradox might arise in a simple case with just three alternatives? We want to describe preferences such that if people vote their preferences and simple majority voting is applied to those votes then x beats y, y beats z and z beats x. Now an obvious way for this to occur would be for all individuals to prefer x to y, y to z and z to x. But social choice theory has many of its origins in microeconomic theory where modeling of individual decision-making always assumes preferences that have a kind of internal consistency: if one alternative is preferred to a second while the second is preferred to a third, then the first is preferred to the third. So we are going to rule out explanations based on preferences that violate this assumption. We want to explain how a voting paradox might arise on three alternatives when individual preferences display this internal consistency.

Suppose there are three individuals. Individual #1 prefers x to y, y to z and so, by our consistency requirement, x to z. Individual #2 prefers y to z, z to x and so y to x. Finally, individual #3 prefers z to x, x to y and so z to y. Then if all individuals straightforwardly vote their preferences, x beats y by 2-to-1 with #1 and #3 voting for x; y beats z with #1 and #2 making up a majority. Finally, z beats x, the winning coalition consisting of #2 and #3. A voting paradox occurs.

We will have occasion many times in this book to describe an assignment of preferences like this. Our technique will be to display a preference ordering by listing alternatives on a single text line with alternatives preferred to any alternatives appearing to their right. Thus, instead of saying #1 prefers x to y, y to z and so x to z, we simply write

$$1: xyz.$$

In this notation, the voting paradox has occurred at a situation like

$$1: xyz$$
$$2: yzx$$
$$3: zxy.$$

The possibility of voting paradoxes has been discovered and rediscovered many times in the last two centuries.

Exercises.

33. There is nothing special here about it being bare majority vote. Suppose one alternative x beats another y only if *more than twice as many* vote for x as vote for y. If there are enough alternatives, we can still get a voting cycle. Show that at the situation

$$1: xyzw$$
$$2: yzwx$$
$$3: zwxy$$
$$4: wxyz$$

x defeats y, y beats z, z beats w and w in turn defeats x. We can't get a cycle like this with just three alternatives – see Exercise 43.

34. Let's pursue the theme of Exercise 33 to an extreme. Suppose one alternative x beats another y only if everyone or almost everyone $(n-1)$ votes for x and at most one votes for y. If there are as many alternatives as individuals, we still get a voting cycle. Show that at the situation

$$1: x_1x_2...x_{n-1}x_n$$
$$2: x_2...x_{n-1}x_nx_1$$
$$\vdots$$
$$n-1: x_{n-1}x_nx_1...x_{n-2}$$
$$n: x_nx_1x_2...x_{n-1}$$

that x_1 defeats x_2, x_2 beats x_3, ..., x_{n-1} defeats x_n and then x_n in turn beats x_1.

35. At an opposite extreme, minority voting can get you in trouble even if there are only two alternatives. Suppose one alternative beats another if 40% or more vote for the first. At

$$1: xy$$
$$2: xy$$
$$3: yx$$
$$4: yx$$
$$5: yx$$

show x beats y and y also beats x. In general, the larger the fraction it takes to win, the more alternatives you must have to get a voting cycle.

How *likely* is a voting paradox? This is not a question with a clear-cut answer. Our voting paradox illustrative example has very heterogeneous preferences, e.g., each individual's most-preferred alternative differs from everyone else's. If two of the three individuals agree on what is their topmost alternative, then that alternative will be a Condorcet winner. More generally, consensus enhances the likelihood of Condorcet winner existence. But social scientists don't know enough about how preferences are formed in different groups to be able to help us figure out the empirical likelihood of voting paradoxes. Worse, we can't determine what fraction of historical situations have failed to have a Condorcet winner because usually we don't collect full preference information.

In the face of these difficulties, the likelihood of a voting paradox has most frequently been estimated in a formal counting way. We count the number of possible assignments of preferences, see what fraction of these lead to a voting paradox and take that fraction to be an estimate of voting paradox likelihood. In order to do this, then, we have to do some counting and this requires learning some basic counting rules. These will come into play again in Chapter 6.

The *fundamental counting rule* works like this: Suppose that carrying out some act can be done in two stages; there are m different ways of carrying out the first stage and for each of these ways of carrying out the first stage there are n ways of carrying out the second stage; then the full act can be carried out in exactly $m \cdot n$ (m times n) ways. To see an illustration of this, let's see how many two letter "words" (possibly nonsensical) can be constructed from an alphabet of 26 letters: a, b, ..., y, z. Writing out a two-letter word is done in two stages: writing the first letter then writing the second. Here there are 26 ways of writing the first letter, 26 ways of carrying out the first stage. Now suppose the first letter is, say, "k" and we now have to carry out the second stage, adding a second letter. "k" can be followed by any of 26 letters. The same is true no matter which letter was selected at the first stage. For each of the 26 ways of carrying out the first stage there are 26 ways of carrying out the second stage; so there are $26 \cdot 26 = 676$ different two letter "words" ranging from "aa" and "ab" down to "zz".

Exercises.
36. Suppose we impose the rule that the second letter has to be chosen so as to be different from the first. Then how many two letter "words" can be constructed?
37. How many two digit numbers are there? (Hint: Be careful; 01 is not a two-digit number but 10 is.)

This rule generalizes so that, for example, if an act can be carried out in three stages with l ways of carrying out the first stage, m ways of carrying out the second stage (for each way of carrying out the first stage) and n ways of carrying out the third stage (for each of the ways of carrying out the first two stages), then the complete action can be carried out in $l \cdot m \cdot n$ ways.

Exercises.
38. How many three letter "words" are there if there is no restriction on repetitions of a letter?
39. How many three letter "words" are there if no letter can be used more than once in a word?
40. How many three digit numbers are there?
41. Suppose you have a standard poker deck of 52 different cards. How many different hands of exactly two cards are there? (Hint: The answer is not $52 \cdot 51$ because, for example, dealing first the ace of spades and then the two of hearts yields the same hand as when dealing first the two of hearts and then dealing the ace of spades.)
42. How many different hands of exactly five cards are there with a standard poker deck?

Now let's take this basic counting rule back to our question of the likelihood of a voting paradox. We will do this where there are three alternatives: x, y and z; three individuals: #1, #2 and #3; and all individuals have preferences that are internally consistent and strong (i.e., no two distinct alternatives are perceived as indifferent; either one is strictly preferred to the other or the other is strictly preferred to the first). First, how many possible preferences are there? Describing a preference on three alternatives can be done in three stages: first stipulate the top-most or best alternative, then stipulate the next-best alternative and then stipulate the worst alternative. The first stage can be done in three ways: either x, y or z can be best. Once an alternative has been selected to be best, there are two alternatives that can be selected in the second stage to be next best. So for each way of carrying out the first stage there are two ways of carrying out the second. Once the top two alternatives have been chosen, there is just one alternative left to be stipulated as the worst. There is just one way of carrying out the third stage for each way of carrying out the first two.

Altogether, then, a preference can be described in $3 \cdot 2 \cdot 1 = 6$ ways. These six internally consistent strong preferences on $\{x, y, z\}$ are

xyz	yxz	zyx
xzy	yzx	zyx.

The next step is to determine how many ways there are of assigning these preferences to individuals. Such an assignment will take place in three stages: an assignment of a preference ordering to the first individual, then to the second individual, then to the third. There are six ways of carrying out each independent stage and so the full assignment can be carried out in $6 \cdot 6 \cdot 6 = 216$ ways. We have seen one of these that gives a voting paradox:

$$1: xyz$$
$$2: yzx$$
$$3: zxy$$

and can easily find an assignment that doesn't give a voting paradox, that does have a Condorcet winner, say:

$$1: yxz$$
$$2: yzx$$
$$3: zyx$$

where y beats both x and z by 2-to-1. Of the 216 assignments, how many yield a voting paradox? It is necessary to go through all 216 cases, applying simple majority voting to each of the three pairs of alternatives and then checking each of the three alternatives to see if it is a Condorcet winner. The result of such a chore is the discovery of 12 voting paradox cases making up a fraction

$$(12/216) = 0.05555\ldots$$

of the total, so that Condorcet winners are found on a fraction 0.94444....

If we had started with more individuals or more than three alternatives we would have ended up with a different fraction. In Table 1, these fractions have been calculated for small odd numbers of individuals and alternatives. Even num-

Table 1

The Number of Individuals	The Number of Alternatives											
	3	5	7	9	11	13	15	17	19	21	23	25
3	0.94444	0.84000	0.76120	0.70108	0.65356	0.61481	0.58249	0.55495	0.53111	0.51021	0.49168	0.47511
5	0.93056	0.80048	0.70424	0.63243	0.57682	0.53235	0.45983	0.46521	0.43908	0.41647	0.39667	0.37915
7	0.92498	0.78467	0.68168	0.60551	0.54703	0.50063	0.46280	0.43128	0.406	0.382	0.362	0.345
9	0.92202	0.77628	0.66976	0.59135	0.534	0.486	0.447	0.415	0.388	0.365	0.345	0.327
11	0.92019	0.77108	0.664	0.585	0.524	0.475	0.436	0.401	0.377	0.351	0.334	0.316
13	0.91893	0.76753	0.659	0.578	0.517	0.468	0.429	0.397	0.369	0.346	0.326	0.309
15	0.91802	0.76496	0.655	0.574	0.512	0.463	0.424	0.391	0.364	0.341	0.321	0.304
17	0.91733	0.76300	0.642	0.570	0.508	0.459	0.420	0.387	0.360	0.337	0.317	0.300
19	0.91678	0.76146	0.650	0.568	0.505	0.456	0.417	0.384	0.357	0.334	0.314	0.297
21	0.91635	0.76023	0.648	0.566	0.503	0.454	0.414	0.382	0.354	0.331	0.311	0.294
23	0.91599	0.75920	0.646	0.564	0.501	0.451	0.412	0.379	0.352	0.329	0.309	0.292
25	0.91568	0.75835	0.645	0.562	0.499	9.450	0.410	0.378	0.351	0.328	0.308	0.290
27	0.91543	0.75763	0.644	0.561	0.498	0.448	0.409	0.376	0.349	0.326	0.306	0.289
29	0.91521	0.75700	0.643	0.560	0.497	0.447	0.407	0.375	0.348	0.325	0.305	0.288
31	0.91501	0.75646	0.642	0.559	0.496	0.446	0.406	0.374	0.347	0.324	0.304	0.287
33	0.91484	0.75598	0.642	0.448	0.495	0.445	0.405	0.373	0.346	0.323	0.303	0.286
35	0.91470	0.75556	0.641	0.557	0.494	0.444	0.405	0.372	0.345	0.322	0.302	0.285
37	0.91456	0.754	0.640	0.557	0.493	0.444	0.404	0.371	0.344	0.321	0.301	0.284
39	0.91444	0.754	0.640	0.556	0.492	0.443	0.403	0.371	0.344	0.321	0.304	0.283
41	0.91434	0.753	0.639	0.556	0.492	0.442	0.403	0.370	0.343	0.320	0.300	0.283
43	0.91424	0.753	0.639	0.555	0.491	0.442	0.402	0.369	0.342	0.319	0.299	0.282
45	0.91415	0.753	0.639	0.555	0.491	0.441	0.401	0.369	0.342	0.319	0.299	0.282
47	0.91407	0.753	0.638	0.554	0.490	0.441	0.401	0.369	0.341	0.318	0.299	0.281
49	0.91399	0.752	0.638	0.554	0.490	0.440	0.401	0.368	0.341	0.318	0.298	0.281
Limit	0.91226	0.74869	0.63082	0.54547	0.48129	0.43131	0.39127	0.35844	0.33100	0.30771	0.28768	0.27025

[a] Five decimal place entries are exact and three decimal place entries are approximations.

bers of *individuals* can generate ties which complicate the counting. That even numbers of *alternatives* must be treated differently is illustrated by the next good but difficult problem.

Exercise.

43. Show that with three individuals and four alternatives a voting paradox never occurs; there is always a Condorcet winner.

Even a cursory examination of Table 1 shows that the fraction of situations with a Condorcet winner decreases with an increase in either the number of individuals or the number of alternatives. Of course this table doesn't *prove* that the decreasing continues with larger numbers. Obtaining a proof of this claim or finding a counterexample is one of the oldest unsolved problems in social choice theory.

Further Reading

On the discovery of the voting paradox and other early history of social choice, there is a historical part in Duncan Black's *The Theory of Committees and Elections* (Cambridge University Press, 1958). For more on the calculation of the likelihood of the voting paradox, see William Gehrlein's, "Condorcet's Paradox, " *Theory and Decision*, Vol. 15 (1983), pp. 161–197, from which Table 1 was obtained.

Chapter 3. Single-Peakedness

Now we know the principle difficulty with the Condorcet winner extension of simple majority voting: *sometimes* it simply doesn't work. On the other hand, it often does work. In Chapter 2 it was suggested that simple majority voting will yield a Condorcet winner if there is sufficient "consensus" among the preference orderings of individuals. In this chapter we will try to capture one notion of "consensus" in a property of preference assignments and show this is sufficient to ensure avoidance of a voting paradox.

Let's return again to the voting paradox example of Chapter 2:

$$1: xyz$$
$$2: yzx$$
$$3: zxy$$

and let's represent this information graphically. We will draw a two-dimensional diagram with the alternatives listed along the horizontal axis (Fig. 3–1).

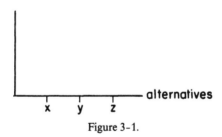

Figure 3–1.

We will represent a preference ordering by a set of points in the diagram, one over each alternative label. If one alternative is preferred to a second, then the point over its label will be drawn higher up in the diagram. Absolute heights are completely irrelevant; only the relative heights of different points play a role (this is why the vertical axis has no units or label). E. g., the ordering 2: yzx is represented by Figures 3–2 and 3–3. Because we wish to use the same diagram simultaneously for several individuals whose dots might otherwise get confused, it is customary to connect points from the same ordering with straight line segments so that 2: yzx would be drawn as in Fig. 3-4.

Be sure you understand that these lines are just visual aids; there are no alternatives *between* x and y on the horizontal axis and so the interior points on the lines connecting points over the labels don't have any preference meaning. The preference graphs for 1: xyz and 3: zxy would be drawn with this same horizontal axis as shown in Figures 3-5 and 3-6.

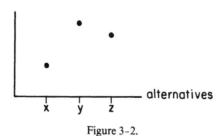

Figure 3-2.

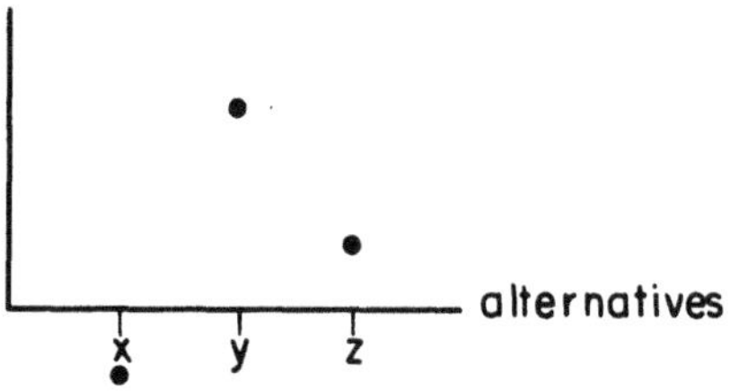

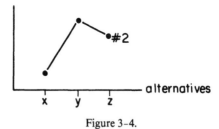

Figure 3-3.

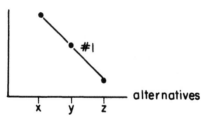

Figure 3-4.

Figure 3-5.

We represent a complete situation with a diagram in which we superimpose the preference graphs of the different individuals. Thus this voting paradox example would appear as Figure 3-7.

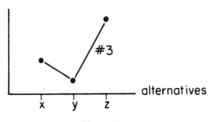

Figure 3-6.

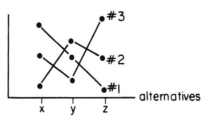

Figure 3-7.

You must be cautious in interpreting such a superimposed diagram; do not try to compare preferences across individuals. Although the dot for #1's most preferred alternative (x) is drawn higher than the dot for #2's most preferred (y), we wouldn't say #1 likes x more than #2 likes y. As we remarked, #1's whole graph could be lowered (even below the axis!) and still preserve the *ordering*. It is also not correct (and for the same reason) to say of Figure 3-7 that #1 likes x more than #2 does (even though #2 likes something more than x and #1 doesn't). Only relative heights within a single individual's graph are ascribed any meaning here.

Notice that in Figure 3-7 *one* of the preference graphs (#3's) has *two peaks,* two points where the graph is at a height greater than at any nearby points. Hold onto this thought as we look at the diagram for a situation where a Condorcet winner exists. We encountered one in the last chapter:

1: yxz
2: yzx
3: zyx.

The diagram for this situation is shown in Figure 3-8.

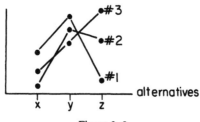

Figure 3-8.

Notice that in this diagram *none* of the preference graphs has two peaks. For this reason we say that the situation

1: yxz
2: yzx
3: zyx

has *single-peaked* preferences.

The central result of this chapter will be that if a situation with an odd number of individuals has a single-peaked preference representation, then there will be a Condorcet winner and thus no voting paradox. To see that this can cover a broader number of situations than it might at first appear, consider the situation

1: zxy
2: zyx
3: yzx

the diagram for this is shown in Figure 3-9.

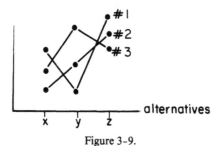

Figure 3-9.

In this diagram, the graph of #1's preferences displays two peaks. But this turns out to be just an artifact of the arbitrary choice we made about the order of x, y and z on the horizontal axis. Suppose we relabeled the axis x, z and y in that order (Fig. 3-10). If we now plot on the new axis the diagram for the situation

1: zxy
2: zyx
3: yzx

that previously gave us two peaks we will get Figure 3-11 which shows single-peaked preferences.

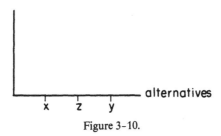

Figure 3-10.

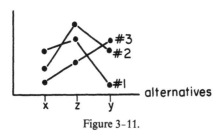

Figure 3-11.

To understand better what we have just done, let us return again to the situation that gave us the voting paradox:

$$1: xyz$$
$$2: yzx$$
$$3: zxy.$$

In our diagram with the order x, y, z on the axis we got the two peaks for #3's preference graph (Fig. 3-12).

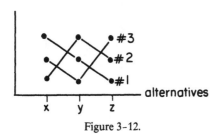

Figure 3-12.

This kind of difficulty does *not* disappear by switching the labels on the horizontal axis to the new x, z, y order (Fig. 3-13). Here there are two peaks for #1's preference graph.

The presence of multiple peaks for someone's preference graph does not disappear with any of the four other possible ways of labeling the horizontal axis (Figs. 3-14, 3-15, 3-16, 3-17).

28

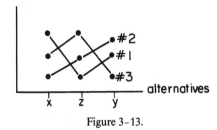

Figure 3-13.

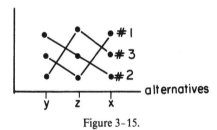

Figure 3-14.

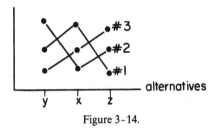

Figure 3-15.

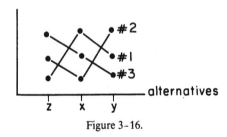

Figure 3-16.

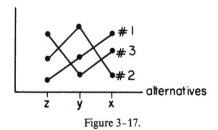

Figure 3-17.

A situation is said to have single-peaked preferences if *for at least one* ordering of alternatives on the horizontal axis of the diagram of the situation none of the graphs of the preferences has more than one peak. Thus for single-peakedness to fail, there must be multiple peaks on *every* possible diagram of the situation.

Exercises.

44. Is the following single-peaked?

$$1: xyz$$
$$2: xyz$$
$$3: yzx$$
$$4: zxy$$

[Hint: You don't have to examine $3 \cdot 2 \cdot 1$ diagrams.]

45. Is the following single-peaked?

$$1: xyzw$$
$$2: yzwx$$
$$3: zwxy$$

[Hint: You don't have to look at $4 \cdot 3 \cdot 2 \cdot 1$ diagrams.]

As we said earlier, we want to show that if a situation with an odd number of individuals displays single-peaked preferences then there will be a Condorcet winner. The reader must be careful to understand that this does *not* mean that if single-peakedness fails then no Condorcet winner exists. What happens when single-peakedness fails depends upon how many individuals have which preference order. The easiest way to see this is to look again at our voting paradox orderings: xyz, yzx and zxy. Suppose instead of three individuals there are 100, that individuals #1 and #2 have the first two orderings respectively. The remaining 98 all have the third ordering, zxy. Obviously, this large group will dominate all simple majority voting outcomes and z will be the Condorcet winner. More generally, *whatever the pattern of all preferences,* if there is a group of half or more of all individuals who have some strong preference ordering in common, then a Condorcet winner will exist.

From *absence* of single-peakedness, then, we are not able to draw a conclusion about voting paradoxes. But from the *presence* of single-peakedness we can conclude no voting paradox occurs. Before we can make progress on proving this result, we must create a rigorous counterpart to our intuitive notion of single-peakedness.

Let Ω be a strict (i.e., no ties) ordering of the elements in X. This Ω ordering is like the list of labels along the horizontal axis in our diagrams. We will define "betweenness" with respect to Ω, B_Ω, as follows, where $B_\Omega(x,y,z)$ is interpreted as "y is between x and z":

$$B_\Omega(x,y,z) \text{ just when either}$$
$$1) \ x \ \Omega \ y \text{ and } y \ \Omega \ z, \text{ or}$$
$$2) \ z \ \Omega \ y \text{ and } y \ \Omega \ x.$$

Notice that since Ω is a strict ordering, $B_\Omega(x,y,z)$ contains implicitly the requirement that x, y and z be all distinct.

30

> *Exercises.*
> 46. $B_\Omega(x,y,z)$ if and only if $B_\Omega(z,y,x)$.
> 47. If x, y and z are all distinct, then *exactly one* of the following must hold:
>
> $$\text{i) } B_\Omega(x,y,z);$$
> $$\text{ii) } B_\Omega(y,x,z);$$
> $$\text{iii) } B_\Omega(x,z,y).$$
>
> 48. Do $B_\Omega(x,y,z)$ and $B_\Omega(y,z,w)$ together imply $B_\Omega(x,y,w)$?

Now let's take this idea of betweenness back to our diagrams. In Figure 3–18, we have alternatives x, y, z and w listed on the horizontal axis in the order xyzw that we will call Ω'

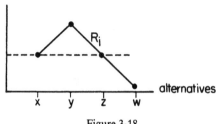

Figure 3-18.

together with a single-peaked preference order, R_i. The "i" decoration on this symbol means that the preference ordering is that of individual i. xR_iz will be read: "individual i finds x to be at least as good as z." xR_iz allows both i being indifferent between x and z and i strictly preferring x to z. If we want to preclude x being indifferent and just say i strictly prefers x to z we write xP_iz. We assume that every individual preference ordering satisfies the internal consistency requirement called *transitivity*: if xR_iy and yR_iz, then xR_iz. Notice that in Figure 3–18

$$xR_iz \text{ and } B_\Omega(x,z,w) \text{ with } xP_iw;$$
$$yR_iz \text{ and } B_\Omega(y,z,w) \text{ with } yP_iw.$$

Generalizing, for every choice of distinct a, b and c,

$$aR_ib \text{ and } B_\Omega(a,b,c) \text{ imply } aP_ic.$$

This is in contrast to Figure 3–19 where we have the same Ω order on the horizontal axis and a preference order, R_j, which is not single-peaked. Here, even though both zR_jy and $B_\Omega(z,y,x)$ are satisfied, we do not have zP_jx.

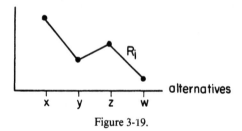

Figure 3-19.

A profile or list of preferences, $u = (R_1, R_2, \ldots, R_n)$ will satisfy *single-peaked preferences* if there exists a strong order Ω such that for *all* i and all distinct alternatives a, b and c in X:

$$aR_ib \text{ and } B_\Omega(a,b,c) \text{ imply } aP_ic.$$

Exercises.

49. Consider the diagram (Fig. 3-20) with a short plateau indicating indifference between y and z.

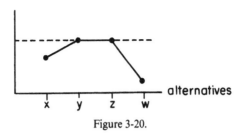

Figure 3-20.

The Ω order is given on the horizontal axis. Is it true here that for all distinct a,b,c that

$$aR_ib \text{ and } B_\Omega(a,b,c) \text{ imply } aP_ic?$$

50. Consider the diagram (Fig. 3-21) with a longer plateau.

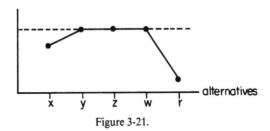

Figure 3-21.

The Ω order is given on the horizontal axis. Is it true here that for all distinct a,b,c that

$$aR_ib \text{ and } B_\Omega(a,b,c) \text{ imply } aP_ic?$$

51. Show that the voter paradox profile

$$1: xyz$$
$$2: yzx$$
$$3: zxy$$

violates our formal single-peaked preferences condition.

52. If a situation s has single-peaked preferences, so does the situation s' that results from eliminating one ordering.

53. If a situation s has single-peaked preferences, so does the situation s' that results by adding an individual with an ordering already in s.
54. If a situation s has single-peaked preferences, so does the situation s' that results by deleting one alternative.

We now want to show that *with an odd number of individuals*, at any profile u that satisfies single-peaked preferences, every finite set of alternatives v has a Condorcet winner. Let's look at a finite set of alternatives v and ask how there can fail to be a Condorcet winner. Reach into v and pull out an alternative, x_1. For this not to be a Condorcet winner, there must be an alternative, x_2, such that x_2 defeats x_1. In analogy with the $N_{+1}(D)$ and $N_{-1}(D)$ notation of Chapter 1, we let $N(xP_iy)$ be the number of individuals $i \in N$ for whom xP_iy at profile $u = (R_1, R_2, ..., R_n)$. Then, since x_2 defeats x_1:

$$N(x_2 P_i x_1) \geq N(x_1 P_i x_2).$$

For x_2 to fail to be a Condorcet winner, there must be an alternative, x_3, that defeats x_2:

$$N(x_3 P_i x_2) \geq N(x_2 P_i x_3).$$

x_3 can't be either x_1 or x_2 (make sure you see why). For x_3 to fail to be a Condorcet winner, there must be an alternative, x_4, that defeats x_3:

$$N(x_4 P_i x_3) \geq N(x_3 P_i x_4).$$

x_4 can't be either x_2 or x_3, but it *can* be x_1 (this is what happens in the classic voting paradox). Continuing in this way, we keep finding another alternative, x_{n+1} in the sequence so that x_{n+1} defeats x_n:

$$N(x_{n+1} P_i x_n) \geq N(x_n P_i x_{n+1}).$$

Since v is finite, eventually x_{n+1} can't be "new", it must have already appeared in the sequence:

$$x_{n+1} = x_m$$

for some m, $1 \leq m < n$. Then we have a cycle:

x_{m+1} defeats x_m, x_{m+2} defeats x_{m+1}, ...,x_n defeats x_{n-1},

$x_m(=x_{n+1})$ defeats x_n.

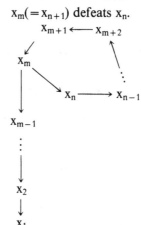

So, it will be sufficient to show that no such cycle can occur under simple majority voting when we have an odd number of individuals and single-peaked preferences. That is, we want to show:

$[(z_2$ defeats $z_1)$ and $(z_3$ defeats $z_2)$ and ... and $(z_t$ defeats $z_{t-1})]$

implies $(z_1$ does not defeat $z_t)$ *or*

$[(z_2$ defeats $z_1)$ and $(z_3$ defeats $z_2)$ and ... and $(z_t$ defeats $z_{t-1})]$

implies $(z_t$ defeats or at least ties $z_1)$.

Of course, while it might seem harder, it would be sufficient to prove the stronger claim

$[(z_2$ defeats or ties $z_1)$ and $(z_3$ defeats or ties $z_2)$ and ... and $(z_t$ defeats or ties $z_{t-1})]$

implies $(z_t$ defeats or at least ties $z_1)$.

But this claim is a consequence of the same claim on just triples:

[(b defeats or ties a) and (c defeats or ties b)]

implies (c defeats or ties a).

Exercise.
55. Use mathematical induction to prove that the claim on triples implies the full claim.

That is, it will be enough to prove that, when the number of individuals is odd and there are single-peaked preferences, the relation "defeats or ties under simple majority voting" has the same kind of internal consistency that we ascribed earlier to individual preferences and called "transitivity."

To prove this, let's assume b defeats or ties a and c defeats or ties b where a, b and c are all distinct:

$$N(bP_ia) \geq N(aP_ib) \text{ and } N(cP_ib) \geq N(bP_ic).$$

By Exercise 47, there are exactly three cases to be considered:

$$B_\Omega(a,b,c), B_\Omega(b,a,c) \text{ or } B_\Omega(a,c,b)$$

where Ω is the order with respect to which we get single-peakedness. In each case we must simply plow our way through some calculations.

Case 1. $B_\Omega(a,b,c)$.
By single-peakedness, cP_ib implies bP_ia. Remembering that R_i is transitive, this tells us cP_ib implies cP_ia. Hence

$$N(cP_ia) \geq N(cP_ib) \tag{1}$$

Also, since c defeats or ties b,

$$N(cP_ib) \geq N(bP_ic). \tag{2}$$

Finally, by single-peakedness, cR_ib implies bP_ia. Again exploiting the transitivity of R_i, this tells us cR_ib implies cP_ia. So,

$$(\text{not } cP_ia) \text{ implies } (\text{not } cR_ib), \text{ i.e., } bP_ic.$$

In particular, aP_ic implies bP_ic. Hence

$$N(bP_ic) \geq N(aP_ic). \tag{3}$$

Combining (1), (2) and (3),

$$N(cP_ia) \geq N(aP_ic),$$

i.e., c defeats or ties a, as we wished to show.

Case 2. $B_\Omega(a,c,b)$.

By single-peakedness, aR_ic implies cP_ib. By transitivity of R_i, aR_ic implies aP_ib. Hence

$$N(aP_ib) \geq N(aR_ic).$$

But $N/2 \geq N(aP_ib)$ since b defeats or ties a. Therefore, $N/2 \geq N(aR_ic)$. In particular,

$$N/2 \geq N(aP_ic). \tag{4}$$

But $N(cP_ia) = N - N(aR_ic)$ and since $N(aR_ic) \leq N/2$,

$$N - N(aR_ic) \leq N - N/2 = N/2.$$

Thus,

$$N(cP_ia) \geq N/2. \tag{5}$$

Combining (4) and (5),

$$N(cP_ia) \geq N(aP_ic),$$

i.e., c defeats or ties a, as we wished to show.

Case 3. $B_\Omega(b,a,c)$.

Suppose we were to try here the same kind of calculations that we carried out in Case 2. cR_ia implies aP_ib by single-peakedness.

$$N(aP_ib) \geq N(cR_ia).$$

But $N/2 \geq N(aP_ib)$ since b doesn't defeat a. Combining,

$$N/2 \geq N(cR_ia).$$

But this means a defeats or at least ties c and that is the *opposite* of what we wish to get! We resolve this by showing that Case 3 simply *can't occur* if the number of individuals is odd.

Single-peakedness gives (bR_ia implies aP_ic) which combines with transitivity of R_i to yield bR_ia implies bP_ic. Hence

$$N(bP_ic) \geq N(bR_ia).$$

But c defeats b, so $N(bP_ic) \leq N/2$. Combining these,

$$N(bR_ia) \leq N/2. \tag{6}$$

But b defeats a so

$$N(bR_ia) \geq N/2. \tag{7}$$

Combining (6) and (7),

$$N(bR_ia) = N/2.$$

Therefore, $N/2$ is an integer, or, what comes to the same thing, N is even. ∎

Exercises.
56. Let v be a subset of X. We will say that a profile $u = (R_1, R_2, ..., R_n)$ satisfies single-peaked preferences *on v* if there is a strong order $\Omega(v)$ *of v* such that for all i and all distinct alternatives a, b and c *in v:*

$$aR_ib \text{ and } B_{\Omega(v)}(a,b,c) \text{ imply } aP_ic.$$

Show that if a profile is single-peaked on X then it is single-peaked on every proper subset of X. The next exercise shows that the converse does not hold.
57. Show that the following profile is not single-peaked on $X = \{x, y, z, w\}$ but that it *is* single peaked on all four triples, $v_1 = \{x, y, z\}$, $v_2 = \{x, y, w\}$, $v_3 = \{x, z, w\}$ and $v_4 = \{y, z, w\}$.

$$1: wyzx$$
$$2: zxyw$$
$$3: yzxw$$

58. Show that there is a Condorcet winner from $\{x, y, z, w\}$ at the profile of the preceding exercise. Examination of the text will show that we didn't need full single-peakedness to get Condorcet winner existence, only single-peakedness on every triple.

Further Reading

Single-peaked preferences were introduced by Duncan Black in *The Theory of Committees and Elections* (Cambridge University Press, 1958). The proof of the theorem in this chapter follows Kenneth J. Arrow, *Social Choice and Individual Values* (Wiley, 1951). For more general sufficient conditions for avoiding the voting paradox, see Prasanta Pattanaik, *Voting and Collective Choice* (Cambridge University Press. 1971).

Chapter 4. Chaos

Without some special combination of circumstances, like single-peakedness, we have seen that a Condorcet winner may fail to exist with simple majority voting. But suppose we have a large $X = \{x_1, x_2, x_3, x_4, \ldots\}$, suppose that the first three alternatives, x_1, x_2 and x_3 are quite similar to one another, and that simple majority voting yields a pattern of results like

A cycle exists among x_1, x_2 and x_3, but these are quite similar to one another and beat everything else. Then the absence of a Condorcet winner doesn't seem very serious: we can just arbitrarily pick one from among the first three alternatives. But we will learn in this chapter that this example is quite atypical; when a Condorcet winner fails to exist, there are multiple cycles. In fact, almost any two alternatives are pieces in a common cycle. Put differently, if there is no Condorcet winner, then for almost all pairs of alternatives x, y, there is a sequence of alternatives, a_1, a_2, ..., a_r such that

$$x = a_1 \text{ loses to } a_2 \text{ which loses to } \ldots \text{ which loses to } a_r = y.$$

Since we are claiming that this works generally also for a sequence, b_1, b_2, ..., b_t leading from y to x:

$$y = b_1 \text{ loses to } b_2 \text{ which loses to } \ldots \text{ which loses to } b_t = x$$

we see x and y as two pieces in a common cycle. The resulting possibility for the rule to wander around in cycles among essentially all possible alternatives is the "chaos" of the title.

Rather than provide rigorous proofs, we will illustrate this result in several ways. We will start with a standard example of non-existence of a Condorcet winner; the pure distribution problem we first discussed in Chapter 2. Suppose there are $n \geq 3$ individuals and one perfectly divisible commodity of which a total of $M > 0$ units are available. An "alternative" will be a distribution of the commodity among the individuals, an *assignment*

$$(z_1, z_2, ..., z_n)$$

where each $z_i \geq 0$ and $z_1 + z_2 + ... + z_n = M$.

Exercises.

59. At least one z_i must be strictly positive.

60. Each $z_i \leq M$.

61. If $(z_1, z_2, ..., z_n) \neq (z_1', z_2', ..., z_n')$, then for at least one i, $z_i' > z_i$.

We assume individuals rank alternatives in a strictly selfish way, preferring those assignments that yield them personally larger amounts. If $n = 4$, $M = 10$ and $x = (1, 2, 3, 4)$, $y = (2, 2, 6, 0)$ then individuals #1 and #3 prefer y to x, #4 prefers x to y and #2 is indifferent between them.

Given this structure on alternatives, together with our selfishness assumption on preferences, it is easy to see that there is no Condorcet winner. For consider potential candidate assignment

$$x = (z_1, z_2, ..., z_n).$$

By Exercise 59, at least one z_i is strictly positive. For notational convenience, assume $z_1 > 0$. Then look at a new alternative x' that takes everything away from #1 and evenly divides his old share among the rest:

$$x' = (z_1', z_2', ..., z_n')$$

where

$$z_1' = 0 \text{ and}$$
$$z_i' = z_i + z_1/(n-1) \text{ for } 2 \leq i \leq n.$$

Then clearly x loses to x' by $n - 1$ to 1 under simple majority vote and so x can not be a Condorcet winner. Since this was done for *arbitrary* x, there is *no* Condorcet winner.

What we want to show is that in this framework we can, through a sequence of majority votes, get from any alternative x to almost any other alternative y. Let's illustrate this again with $n = 4$, $M = 10$

$$x = (4, 2, 2, 2) \text{ and } y = (0, 0, 1, 9).$$

Now clearly y can't beat x under simple majority vote (x would win 3-to-1). But consider the sequence

$$a_1 = x = (4, 2, 2, 2)$$
$$a_2 = (5, 3, 0, 2)$$
$$a_3 = (7, 0, \tfrac{1}{2}, 2\tfrac{1}{2})$$
$$a_4 = y = (0, 0, 1, 9).$$

Then a_2 beats x with #1 and #2 voting for a_2 and #3 voting for x; a_3 beats a_2 by 3-to-1 and then a_4 beats a_3 by 2-to-1.

Two observations must be made about this sequencing construction. First it must be made clearly systematic if we are to be certain generally about paths from one arbitrary alternative to another. Second, there are some very special y's such that y can't be reached from x by any sequence.

Exercise.

62. Suppose $x = (4, 2, 2, 2)$ again but that this time $y = (0, 0, 0, 10)$. Show that there is *no* sequence leading from x to y.

What is special about the y in Exercise 62 is that it has only one non-zero entry; for any *other* kind of y and for any x, there is a path from x to y. As noted, to establish this we must find a systematic way of constructing such a path. We will do this first for $n = 3$ and then deal with the general case. So we let $x = (z_1, z_2, z_3)$ be an initial point and $y = (z_1', z_2', z_3') \neq x$ be a final point where at least two z_i' values are positive. Using Exercise 61, let's assume for notational convenience that $z_1' > z_1$. Some other z_i' is positive; assume it is $z_2' > 0$. Using Exercise 60,

$$M \geq z_1' > z_1$$

so $z_i > 0$ for some $i \geq 2$.

Case 1. $z_2 > 0$. Consider taking a little bit, δ ("delta") of the commodity away from #2, giving this to #1 and giving the rest to #3 to get

$$a_2 = (z_1 + \delta, 0, z_3 + z_2 - \delta).$$

This qualifies to be an assignment as long as $\delta \geq 0$ and $\delta \leq z_2 + z_3$. Further, a_2 will beat x if $\delta > 0$ and $\delta < z_2$. In turn, a_2 will lose to y if δ is chosen so that $\delta < z_1' - z_1$ for then #1 will vote for y over a_2 (joining #2 since $z_2' > 0$). The path would be

$$x = a_1 \text{ loses to } a_2 \text{ loses to } a_3 = y$$

assuming δ is chosen to satisfy

$$0 < \delta < \min \{z_2, z_1' - z_1\}.$$

Case 2. $z_2 = 0$, $z_3 > 0$. This time we will take a bit, δ, away from #3, giving half to each of #1 and #2:

$$a_2 = (z_1 + \delta/2, \delta/2, z_3 - \delta).$$

This qualifies to be an assignment as long as $\delta \geq 0$ and $\delta \leq z_3$. Further, a_2 will beat x if $\delta > 0$ and $\delta < z_3$. Now a_2 will lose to y if also

$$\delta/2 < z_1' - z_1$$

so #1 will vote for y over a_2 and if also

$$\delta/2 < z_2'$$

so that #2 will vote for y over a_2. So the path will be

$$x = a_1 \text{ loses to } a_2 \text{ loses to } a_3 = y$$

when δ is chosen to satisfy

$$0 < \delta < \min \{z_1' - z_1, z_2', z_3\}.$$

Now let's extend this reasoning from the three individual situation to the general $n \geq 3$ case. Having dealt with $n = 3$, we may now suppose that $n \geq 4$. Let $x = (z_1, z_2, \ldots, z_n)$ and $y = (z_1', z_2', \ldots, z_n')$ where at least two z_i' values are positive; we wish to show there is a path from x to y. Let i and j be two individuals with smallest amounts in y:

$$\left. \begin{array}{c} z_i' \leq z_k' \\ \\ z_j' \leq z_k' \end{array} \right\} \text{ for all } k \neq i \text{ or } j.$$

Our path will be composed of two path sections.

Path Section 1. We are going to systematically pile up everything on i and j. Let everyone else be relabeled $1^*, 2^*, \ldots, (n-2)^*$ and let m^* be the first in this new label sequence who got a non-zero assignment at x:

$$z_{1^*} = 0, z_{2^*} = 0, \ldots, z_{(m-1)^*} = 0, z_{m^*} > 0.$$

At the first step in Path Section 1, we leave $1^*, 2^*, \ldots, (m-1)^*$ alone, take z_{m^*}, divide it into $n - m^*$ equal pieces and give these to $(m+1)^*, \ldots, (n-2)^*$, i and j. At the next step we leave $1^*, 2^*, \ldots, (m-1)^*, m^*$ alone, take

$$z_{(m+1)^*} + z_{m^*}/(n-m^*) \quad (> 0)$$

divide it into $n - m^* - 1$ equal pieces and give these to $(m+2)^*, \ldots, (n-2)^*$, i and j. We continue in this way until we reach

$$z = (0, 0, \ldots, 0, c_i, 0, \ldots, 0, c_j, 0, \ldots, 0),$$

with c_i and c_j both positive.

To illustrate this, suppose $n = 5$, $M = 10$, $x = (0, 3, 3, 3, 1)$ and $y = (0, 0, 9, 1, 0)$. Arbitrarily pick two from among the three individuals getting least (zero) at y; say $i = 5, j = 2$,

$$1^* = 1$$
$$2^* = 3$$
$$3^* = 4.$$

Then the steps of Stage 1 give

$$a_2 = (0, 4, 0, 4, 2)$$
$$a_3 = (0, 6, 0, 0, 4).$$

Clearly, the alternative created at each step in this stage beats the one just before it under simple majority voting since only one votes for the earlier and at least two (e.g., i and j) vote for the new.

Path Section 2. Remember that i and j were were chosen so that z_i' and z_j' were minimal. If both $z_i' \geq c_i$ and $z_j' \geq c_j$ we would have

$$\sum z_k' > z_i' + z_j' \geq c_i + c_j = M$$

contrary to the fact that y is an allocation of M units. Because of this contradiction we can't have *both* $z_i' \geq c_i$ and $z_j' \geq c_j$.

Case 1. One of these inequalities does hold. Suppose $z_i' \geq c_i$ but $c_j > z_j'$ (see the 5-person example in the Path Section 1 discussion). Then in a vote between z and y, only j would vote for z, i would not and at least two others would vote for y (remember at least two have $z_k' > 0$ and since z_i' and z_j' are minimal, $z_k' > 0$ for at least two *other than* i and j). So for this case, the path ends with

$$z = a_{r-1} \text{ loses to } a_r = y.$$

Case 2. $c_i > z_i'$ and $c_j > z_j'$. We will go from z to one intermediate alternative w and then go to y. Define

$$s = (c_i - z_i') + (c_j - z_j') > 0$$

and

$$F = (c_i - z_i')/s.$$

Of the total amount s that must be reallocated from i and j in going from z to y, a fraction F will be reallocated in going from z to w. It will all be taken from i and everyone other than i and j will get the fraction F of what they receive at y; j is left alone:

$$w = (F \cdot z_1', \ldots, F \cdot z_{i-1}', z_i', F \cdot z_{i+1}', \ldots,$$
$$F \cdot z_{j-1}', c_j, F \cdot z_{j+1}', \ldots, F \cdot z_n')$$

While i votes for z over w, at least two in N-{i, j} vote for w over z and w wins. w then loses to y (j votes for w while at least two in N-{i, j} vote for y). ∎

Exercises.

63. With 10 individuals, show a sequence of majority votes that will get from

$$(2, 1, 0, 1, 1, 1, 1, 1, 1, 1)$$
to $$(0, 0, 0, 0, 0, 0, 0, 0, 5, 5).$$

64. What is the *shortest* sequence that will work for Exercise 63?

So, in the pure distribution case, where there is no Condorcet winner, if we ignore the extreme allocations where one person gets everything, then we can get from any one alternative to any other by means of a sequence of simple majority votes.

To illustrate this idea in a different context let's look at another familiar kind of situation where a Condorcet winner doesn't exist. Suppose X is the closed interval from 0 to 10. There are three individuals whose preferences are as indicated in Figure 4-1. Be careful that you see how this diagram differs from those in Chapter 3. Here there is a continuum of alternatives and all parts of the graphed lines represent preferences; in Chapter 3 lines connecting points were just visual aids and did not themselves represent preferences.

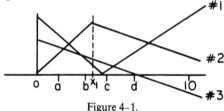

Figure 4-1.

Single-peakedness is violated here but we must still check to see if there is a Condorcet winner. (Remember our Chapter 3 theorem told us single-peakedness was *sufficient* for a Condorcet winner but did *not* tell us it was *necessary*.) But consulting Figure 4-1, we see that everything in $(x_1, 10]$ loses to x_1, that everything in $(0, x_1]$ loses to 0 while 0 loses to 10. There is no Condorcet winner.

These same observations show that if x and y are any two alternatives in $[0, 10]$ we can get from x to y by a sequence of simple majority votes. For example, we can get from c to d by going from c to x_1 to 0 to 10 to d.

Exercise.

65. Show a path from a to b; from b to a.

As a transitional illustration, let's modify the previous example by changing the set, X, of alternatives from the closed interval $[0, 10]$ to the whole real line. Individual #1 will still always prefer smaller to larger values. Individual #2 will most prefer 10 and will like other alternatives less in a way determined by the distance from 10 with alternatives closer to 10 more preferred:

$$xP_2y \text{ if and only if } |x-10| \leq |y-10|.$$

Individual #3 least likes 5, prefers other alternatives more the farther they are from 5:

$$xP_3y \text{ if and only if } |x-5| \geq |y-5|.$$

All this information is represented in Figure 4-2.

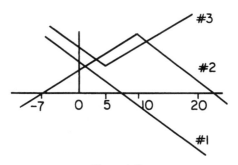

Figure 4-2.

Exercise.
66. There is no Condorcet winner in this situation.

As there is no Condorcet winner, we now start to see if we can get from any one alternative to any other. For example, could we get from 10 to 20 even though a majority prefer 10 to 20? The path will have to go well away from these two alternatives. Consider -7. Certainly #1 prefers -7 to $+10$. So does #3 since -7 is farther from 5 than 10 is. So 10 loses to -7. But -7 loses to 20 since 20 is preferred to -7 by #3 (20 is farther from 5 than -7 is) and also by #2 (20 is closer to 10 than -7 is).

Our final illustration serves both to reinforce the theme of getting from any place to any other place when there is no Condorcet winner but also reveals the importance of the one-dimensionality facet of our definition of single-peakedness in the previous Chapter. We will suppose X is the whole two-dimensional Cartesian plane (Fig. 4–3).

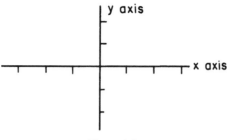

Figure 4-3.

Now just as in Figures 4–1 and 4–2 we used two dimensions to represent preferences over a one-dimensional alternative space, so here we might use three dimensions to represent preferences over a two-dimensional alternative space. Figure 4–4 shows a preference surface with a "single-peak" for this case analogous to the preference curves in Figures 4–1 and 4–2.

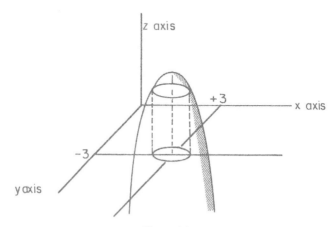

Figure 4-4.

But with several individuals, these three-dimensional diagrams become clumsier than are two-dimensional diagrams which represent surfaces by contour lines. The preferences in Figure 4–4 would yield the contour map of Figure 4–5. This individual is indifferent between any two points on a contour line and prefers points closer to the center to those more distant.

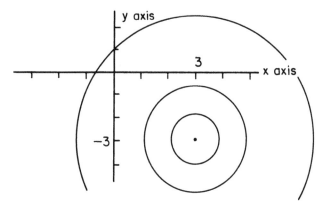

Figure 4-5.

For pictorial simplicity, we will work with preferences that not only show "single peaks" but also have circular contour lines. Since circles represent the locus of points of equal distance, we are working with cases where preferences can be represented by distance. Individual i has a most preferred alternative x_i and preferences based on the distance $d(x, x_1)$ of an alternative x from alternative x_i:

$$xP_iy \text{ if and only if } d(x, x_i) < d(y, x_i).$$

More distant alternatives are less preferred.

With these preliminaries, let us again suppose three individuals, this time with most preferred alternatives given by

$$x_1 = (4, 2)$$
$$x_2 = (8, 4)$$
$$x_3 = (6, -1).$$

In Figure 4-6 is a diagram showing the location of these peaks, the location of one additional, arbitrarily chosen point, $A = (6, 2)$ and the contour lines for each individual through A.

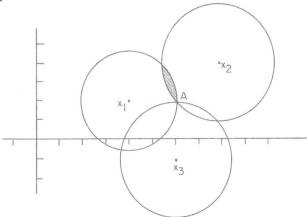

Figure 4-6.

The connection between the diagrams and majority voting becomes clearer by focusing on the shaded region. These are points that are closer to *both* x_1 and x_2 than A is and so represent alternatives that both #1 and #2 strictly prefer to A. Thus the interior of the shaded region constitutes all alternatives that would beat A by simple majority voting because of the coalition of #1 and #2. Similarly, the interior of the overlap of the two other pairs of circles will show all alternatives that would beat A by simple majority voting because of other majority coalitions. In Figure 4–7, then, the interior of the shaded region represents *all* alternatives that could beat A by simple majority voting.

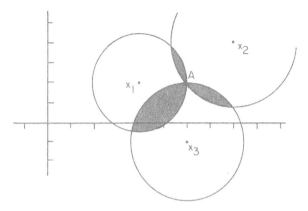

Figure 4–7.

The reader might guess that in a nice example like this where preferences have unique local maxima, i.e., "single peaks" and have simple, circular indifference sets, that a Condorcet winner will exist. But that is not correct. Single-peakedness as defined in Chapter 2 was along *one* dimension. The "single peak" phenomenon we observe here relates to a two-dimensional alternative space and does not guarantee a Condorcet winner. Of course, it *may* happen that preferences are such that a voting paradox is avoided; as an extreme case, if everyone's best alternative were identical, it would be a Condorcet winner. A more interesting example is found in the following problem.

45

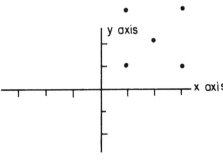

Exercise.
67. Consider Figure 4-8, with five individuals, circle-contour preferences and
    best points

$$x_1 = (2, 2), \qquad x_2 = (1, 1), \qquad x_3 = (1, 3)$$
$$x_4 = (3, 3), \qquad x_5 = (3, 1).$$

Figure 4-8.

Show that the point x_1 at #1's peak is also a Condorcet winner.

But for our Figure 4-6 and 4-7 example, no Condorcet winner exists. To see
this, examine Figure 4-9 where we have added in the lines through each of the pairs
of best points.

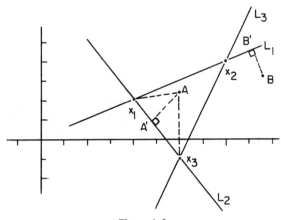

Figure 4-9.

Since the best points are not collinear (i.e., there is no line passing through all
three best points) it must be true of *any* point in the plane that it is not on at least one
of the lines L_1, L_2 or L_3. Some points, like A and B in Figure 4-9 are not on any of
the lines. To see that A, for example, is not a Condorcet winner, construct a line
from A perpendicular to one of the lines, say L_2, where it intersects at point A'. As
Figure 4-9 shows, the line segment x_1A' is one side of a right triangle of which x_1A

is the hypotenuse. Since in any right triangle the hypotenuse is the longest side, the distance of A' from x_1 is less than the distance of A from x_1, i.e., individual #1 prefers A' to A. By the same kind of reasoning, #3 prefers A' to A so A would lose to A' under simple majority vote and A can not be a Condorcet winner. All of this is to say that A' must be in the region that is shaded in Figure 4-7. It is precisely the fact that there *is* a shaded region in Figure 4-7 that tells us A is not a Condorcet winner.

The same reasoning works for other points. From point B in Figure 4-9 we construct a perpendicular to L_1 which meets at B'. B' will be preferred to B by both #1 and #2 so that B is not a Condorcet winner.

Nor will points like A' or B', which appear on a line, be Condorcet winners. A' will lose by votes of #2 and #3 to the point on L_3 that is reached by a perpendicular from A'.

Exercises.
68. Find a point on L_3 to which B' loses. Find a point on L_1 to which A' loses.
69. Find points to which each of x_1, x_2 and x_3 lose.
70. Will there ever exist a Condorcet winner if the best points of the three individuals are not collinear?
71. Will there always exist a Condorcet winner if the best points of the three individuals *are* collinear?

Now that we know our example has no Condorcet winner, we might guess from our earlier work in this chapter that there is a path from any alternative to any other. Instead of *proving* this we will merely illustrate it by showing a path to B from A in spite of the fact that *everyone* prefers A to B. To see how we can move away from the peaks, let's look at Figure 4-10. This construction is designed to show that not only would #1 and #3 vote for A' over A=z_1 but for any other alternative in the shaded region including points very close to A*, like z_2. Now that z_2 beats A, we can perform the same kind of move from z_2. Since L_3 is the farthest line from z_2, we carry out the same construction in Figure 4-11. A perpendicular from z_2 meets L_3 at z_2'; if continued the same distance across on the other side we get to z_2^*; coming back just a little we get z_3 which will beat z_2 by 2-to-1 on the votes of #2 and #3.

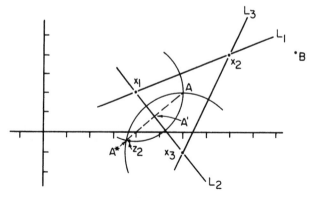

Figure 4-10.

z_3 can then be reflected through L_1 (the farthest line from z_3) to $z_3{}^*$ from which we come back slightly to z_4, which beats z_3 on the votes of #1 and #2. One more reflection, this time of z_4 across L_3 and then slightly back to z_5 (which thus beats z_4) is all that is needed since z_5 will lose to B on the votes of #1 and #2.

Without being rigorous about it, it isn't hard to see that a long enough sequence of reflections can get us arbitrarily far from the three peaks. If this is true, we can reach any alternative y. Just go farther out than y by reflections and then come in (by unanimous vote) to y.

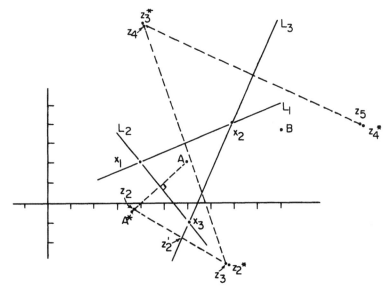

Figure 4-11.

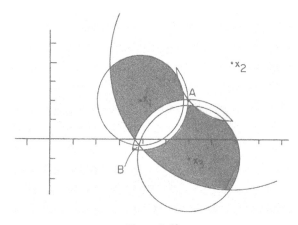

Figure 4-12.

48

For another way of visualizing the claim we are making, examine Figure 4-12, where we have reproduced the peaks, x_1, x_2 and x_3, the initial allocation and the tre-foil shaped set of all alternatives that defeat A directly under simple majority vote (the set that was shaded back in Figure 4-7). One point, B, is selected from the tre-foil set and contour lines are drawn through B.

The shaded regions in this figure are alternatives that do not defeat A directly but do defeat A "indirectly" by defeating B which defeats A. By starting with all possible B's we find all those alternatives that can be reached from A in two but not

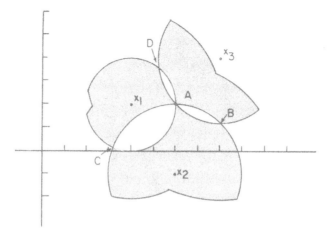

Figure 4-13

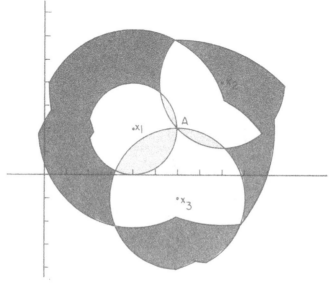

Figure 4-14

one majority votes. Figure 4–13 shows the original trefoil set that could be reached in one vote and then, shaded, the set that can be reached in two but not fewer votes. Figure 4–14 then adds the set of alternatives that can be reached in 3 but not fewer votes. It is the thrust of this chapter that if A is not a Condorcet winner, these sets grow and grow to fill up the entire plane.

Exercise.

72. Illustrate these ideas by constructing the first few reachable sets in the symmetric case where A is the point $(5, \frac{1}{2}\sqrt{3})$ and the three preference peaks are

$$x_1 = (0, 0)$$
$$x_2 = (10, 0)$$
$$x_3 = (5, \sqrt{3})$$

Further Reading

The first results on being able to reach any alternative from a starting point that is not a Condorcet winner were by Richard McKelvey (see e.g., the difficult "General Conditions for Global Intransitivities in Formal Voting Models," *Econometrica*, Vol. 47 (1979), pp. 1085–1111). More recent work has been done by Norman Schofield. See his recent, but also difficult, *Social Choice and Democracy* (Springer-Verlag, 1986).

William Riker interprets these results as quite destructive of the traditional concepts of equilibrium and stability in democratic theory ("topsy-turvy revolution is as certainly predicted as incremental change"); see his *Liberalism Against Populism* (Freeman, 1982). For an introduction to spatial voting theory that includes both the McKelvey work and more general models that seek to explain why we see more incremental change than revolution, read *The Spatial Theory of Voting: An Introduction* by James M. Enelow and Melvin Hinich (Cambridge University Press, 1984).

Chapter 5. Other Voting Extensions

As we first learned in Chapter 2, the central difficulty with the Condorcet winner extension of simple majority voting is that sometimes it doesn't work because no Condorcet winner exists. In this chapter we will consider three alternative extensions that *will* always work.

Suppose now our set X of alternatives is ordered in some arbitrary way that we will indicate by subscript labels on the alternatives;

$$X = \{x_1, x_2, \ldots, x_N\}.$$

Thus x_i precedes x_j in the ordering just when $i < j$. This is the *managing ordering* of the alternatives. Choosing from X now proceeds in stages. At the first stage, a simple majority vote choice is made between x_1 and x_2. The winner is pitted in the second stage against x_3 in a simple majority vote comparison. The third stage is a simple majority vote choice between x_4 and the winner of the second stage. This continues until, at the $N\text{-}1^{st}$ stage, x_N is pitted against the winner of the $N\text{-}2^{nd}$ stage. Unfortunately, this doesn't quite work because "the" winner of a stage isn't clear since ties may be the outcome of a voting decision. To tighten up this definition, we need a rule for breaking ties at each stage (before the last). It won't work even to designate some one individual as tie-breaker; he may be indifferent between a pair of tied alternatives. One way that will work is to use the managing ordering on X. If at any stage a tie occurs, we will break the tie in favor of the lower labeled alternative. While not strictly necessary, it seems natural to extend this tie breaking to the last stage as well so that the set chosen from X will always be a singleton. This method always works, in the sense of not yielding an empty set, because we don't take the winner of the last, $N\text{-}1^{st}$, stage and risk its losing a voting comparison with any alternative (except the one other that was present at the last stage).

Let's see how this works. Suppose we face the situation

$$1: x_1x_2x_4x_3$$
$$2: x_2x_3x_4x_1$$
$$3: x_3x_4x_1x_2$$
$$4: x_4x_2x_3x_1.$$

At the first application of simple majority voting, x_1 and x_2 tie so x_1 wins the first stage. At the second stage, x_3 defeats x_1 by 3-to-1 and encounters x_4 at the third stage. Here there is another tie, this time broken in favor of x_3. x_3 is the alternative chosen. Notice that if x_3 were matched against x_2, then x_2 would win 3-to-1, but that match-up never occurs. It is just because this staging extension *doesn't* consider all possible matchups that it always guarantees a winner.

But we have purchased non-empty choice sets at a fairly high price. This social choice procedure has serious flaws (as might be expected of a rule that totally ignores certain information, like the x_3 vs. x_2 comparison in the previous example). For one such flaw, let us recall that Condorcet winners seemed to us in Chapter 2 to be intuitively natural elements to be chosen – the problem is non-existence. But that does suggest a simple appealing criterion for a social choice procedure: when a Condorcet winner exists, it should be among the elements chosen. Let's take that criterion and examine our staging procedure. Consider the situation

$$1: x_1x_2x_4x_3x_5$$
$$2: x_3x_4(x_1x_2)x_5$$
$$3: x_5x_2x_4x_3x_1$$

where the (x_1x_2) segment in #2's ordering indicates that she is indifferent between x_1 and x_2. Here x_2 is a Condorcet winner: x_2 ties x_1 and beats each of the others by 2-to-1. It is the only Condorcet winner; x_1 loses to x_4 and every other alternative loses to x_2. But applying our new procedure, at the first stage there is a tie between x_1 and x_2 broken in favor of x_1. x_1 then loses to x_3 which loses to x_4 which finally beats x_5; x_4 is chosen. So a first flaw: the staging procedure may fail to choose a Condorcet winner when one is present.

For a second flaw, let's look at a new situation:

$$1: x_2x_1x_4x_3$$
$$2: x_3x_2x_1x_4$$
$$3: x_1x_4x_3x_2.$$

This time x_2 beats x_1, then loses to x_3 which loses to x_4; x_4 is chosen. But *everyone* prefers x_1 to x_4. It seems silly to choose an alternative when another is available that is *unanimously* preferred to the first.

Next we will use this procedure to introduce a quite different aspect of social choice that will play a major role in the next two chapters. So far, at any given situation, we make just one decision: a choice from the set X of all alternatives. Back in Chapter 2 where X contained only two alternatives, this made good sense – there were no proper subsets (see the Mathematical Appendix) of X that could present an interesting choice problem. But when X contains three or more alternatives, this is no longer true. At any given moment, only a proper subset, v, of the alternatives might be available and choice would then have to be made from v, not from all of X.

When we talk about choices made by *individuals*, this presents no new problems: we suppose i has a preference relation R_i over all of X and then when confronted with a set v of available alternatives, $\emptyset \neq v \subset X$, choice is made from v by picking those alternatives that are highest in R_i restricted to v. If i:xy(zw)rt and choice must be made from {z, w, t}, the choice is {z, w}, the two alternatives judged by i to be the (tied) best alternatives from those available.

For choices made through social choice procedures, we need to explicitly extend the choosing process to subsets of X. For the staging procedure there is a natural extension. Rather than give a formal definition (one will appear in Chapter 6), we illustrate the idea at the situation

$$1: x_1x_2x_4x_3$$
$$2: x_2x_3x_4x_1$$
$$3: x_3x_4x_1x_2$$
$$4: x_4x_3x_2x_1.$$

On all of X, x_1 wins a tie break against x_2, then loses to x_3 which wins a tie break against x_4. On a proper subset of X like $v = \{x_2, x_3, x_4\}$, the first stage would pit the two lowest labeled alternatives in v in a simple majority vote comparison. x_2 beats x_3 and goes to the second stage against x_4 where it wins a tie break. x_2 is chosen from v. Clearly, on subsets of just two alternatives this rule chooses just like simple majority voting except that a tie break is added. If we don't use the tie break at the last stage, this procedure is more closely an extension of simple majority voting.

So now let's see a social choice rule as generating a "choosing function" that looks not just at X but also at its non-empty subsets and selects a chosen set from each. We must determine if we want there to be certain relationships among the chosen sets. For example, suppose we interpret the set C(v) chosen from $v \subset X$ as the "best" elements in v. Then a plausible requirement among the chosen sets would be:

If $v \subset v' \subset X$ and $x \in v \cap C(v')$, then $x \in C(v)$.

In words, if x is best in v' and x is in a subset v of v', x must be one of the best in v. This is just the kind of property satisfied when an individual chooses from a set the alternatives highest in his R_i preference ordering restricted to the set.

This consistency property, however, is not satisfied by the extension of our staging procedure as we have already seen at the situation

$$1: x_1x_2x_4x_3$$
$$2: x_2x_3x_4x_1$$
$$3: x_3x_4x_1x_2$$
$$4: x_4x_3x_2x_1.$$

Here we saw x_3 was chosen from $v' = X$ but not from $v = \{x_2, x_3, x_4\}$ where x_2 alone was chosen.

Another flaw in the staging extension of simple majority voting is that it encourages lying. Up until now we have been supposing identity between individuals' internal mental preference ordering and the explicit ordering on a ballot submitted to the social choice procedure. We have assumed truthful revelation of preferences. But suppose we look again at the situation just above. We will assume these are the *true* preferences. As we have seen, x_3 is chosen from X if these true preferences are reported. From the perspective of individual #1, he is getting as outcome an alternative x_3 way down in his ranking. This happens in part because at the second stage x_3 is matched against x_1 which comes out of the first stage in part because #1 voted for x_1 against x_2. This suggests it might benefit #1 to lie to get x_2 to emerge from the first stage. Suppose #1 falsely reports that his ordering is $x_2x_1x_3x_4$ while everyone else reports their true preferences so that the *reported* situation looks like

$$1: x_2x_1x_3x_4$$
$$2: x_2x_3x_4x_1$$
$$3: x_3x_4x_1x_2$$
$$4: x_4x_3x_2x_1.$$

Our procedure then has x_2 beat x_1 in the first stage and then x_2 wins tie breaks against both x_3 and x_4 so x_2 is chosen. Since in his true ordering #1 prefers this outcome to the x_3 that results from honest reporting, the rule has given #1 an incentive to lie.

For a final flaw (as if another is needed!) it must be pointed out that outcomes here are terribly sensitive to the managing ordering on X that serves both as tie breaker and as procedural rule for determining which new alternative is brought in at each stage. For example, let us again examine the classic voter's paradox situation

$$1: abc$$
$$2: bca$$
$$3: cab.$$

If the managing ordering on X is abc, then a goes up against b, winning the first stage and then losing to c at the second stage.

Exercise.
73. If the managing ordering is acb, then b wins; if the managing ordering is cba, then a wins.

This calculation, together with those in Exercise 73, shows that *any* alternative can be chosen depending on the managing ordering. Individuals have an incentive here to waste resources in trying to manipulate the selection of the order in which alternatives are taken up.

By now it is probably clear that this social choice rule has paid an extremely high price for avoiding a few failures of Condorcet winner existence. So let's try something different. The Condorcet winner rule chooses from X those alternatives that beat (or at least tie) all N-1 other alternatives under simple majority voting. Suppose that we instead calculate for each alternative x the number $n(x)$ of other alternatives in X that x beats or at least ties. Then choose from X those alternatives that give a highest value to $n(x)$, those alternatives that win or tie more simple majority vote tests than any other. This rule is easily extended to non-empty subsets v of X. Choose from v those alternatives in v that beat (or tie) under simple majority vote the most alternatives in v. To illustrate this procedure, called the *Copeland rule*, let's look at the situation that gave the staging procedure so much trouble:

$$1: x_1x_2x_3x_4$$
$$2: x_2x_3x_4x_1$$
$$3: x_3x_4x_1x_2$$
$$4: x_4x_3x_2x_1.$$

The Copeland rule is applied to this profile of preferences in the next Exercise.

Exercises.

74. Show that, at the profile of preferences just given, the Copeland rule gives

$$C(\{x_1, x_2, x_3, x_4\}) = \{x_2, x_3\}; \quad C(\{x_1, x_2, x_3\}) = \{x_2, x_3\};$$
$$C(\{x_1, x_2, x_4\}) = \{x_2, x_4\}; \quad C(\{x_1, x_3, x_4\}) = \{x_3\}$$
$$C(\{x_2, x_3, x_4\}) = \{x_2, x_3\}; \quad C(\{x_1, x_2\}) = \{x_1, x_2\}$$
$$C(\{x_1, x_3\}) = \{x_3\}; \quad C(\{x_1, x_4\}) = \{x_4\}$$
$$C(\{x_2, x_3\}) = \{x_2, x_3\}; \quad C(\{x_2, x_4\}) = \{x_2, x_4\}$$
$$C(\{x_3, x_4\}) = \{x_3\}.$$

75. If a Condorcet winner exists, it is chosen under the Copeland rule.
76. If v has *exactly* two alternatives, the Copeland rule makes the same choice as simple majority vote.

The results of Exercises 75 and 76 make it easy to see the Copeland rule as an extension of simple majority voting, and one that avoids at least one flaw of the staging procedure - failing to choose Condorcet winners. The next exercise shows that the Copeland rule avoids another flaw of the staging procedure.

Exercise.

77. Suppose there are two alternatives x and y in the set v and that everyone without exception strictly prefers x to y. Then y is not chosen from v by the Copeland rule.

But not all flaws are avoided. When we were discussing the staging procedure, we saw that we could not interpret the choice function as picking out the "best" alternatives. We saw the staging procedure violated a consistency condition that would follow from such an interpretation:

$$\text{If } v \subset v' \subset X \text{ and } x \in v \cap C(v'), \text{ then } x \in C(v).$$

The Copeland rule also can not be interpreted in this way, but we have to look at finer details than just the consistency condition. We will use Exercise 74 to illustrate the problem involved. For the choice function of Exercise 74, we had $x_4 \in C(\{x_1, x_2, x_4\})$ so if we could use this "best alternative" interpretation, we would say x_4 is at least as good as x_2. Also, $x_2 \in C(\{x_2, x_3\})$ so x_2 is at least as good as x_3. But then we would want to say x_4 is at least as good as x_3. But x_4 is not in $C(\{x_3, x_4\})$.

The Copeland rule also has a flaw of a sort we haven't considered before. Suppose there are 100 voters and the situation we face is

$$
\begin{array}{ll}
1-21: & xyz \\
22-34: & yzx \\
35-40: & zxy \\
41-59: & xzy \\
60-80: & yxz \\
81-100: & zyx.
\end{array}
$$

Suppose these 100 voters are split into two constituencies consisting of the first 40 voters and the remaining 60. If Copeland's rule is applied to the constituency of individuals 1 to 40, the set chosen from {x, y, z} would be {x}. When applied to individuals 41–100, Copeland's rule chooses all of {x, y, z} (you should verify both of these claims). Thus x is chosen in *both* constituencies. But if instead we apply Copeland's rule to all individuals lumped together, the chosen set is {y} (as you should also verify). Under these circumstances some individuals would seem to have strong incentives to waste resources in splitting or merging constituencies.

Now let's examine one more extension of simple majority voting. This is a simpler rule and one that will seem quite familiar to most readers. For a set v of alternatives, associate with each alternative x in v the number of 1st place votes it receives in preference orderings restricted to v, that is, in the orderings restricted to v, the number of top-most indifference sets containing x. Choose the set of alternatives with the highest value of this number. This is the rule of *plurality voting*.

Exercises.

78. If v has exactly two alternatives, the plurality voting rule makes the same choice as simple majority voting.

79. Suppose x and y are in v and everyone unanimously strictly prefers x to y. Then y is not chosen from v by the plurality rule.

80. Use the standard voter's paradox example to show that plurality voting also fails the consistency condition:

$$\text{If } v \subset v' \subset X \text{ and } x \in v \cap C(v'), \text{ then } x \in C(v).$$

81. Construct an example to show that as with Copeland's rule there is an incentive to split or merge constituencies.

82. Show by an example that a Condorcet winner need not be chosen by plurality rule.

Although Exercise 78 tells us that plurality voting on two alternatives coincides with simple majority voting, it gives results on larger sets sharply at variance with the results of simple majority voting (see Exercise 83).

Exercises.

83. Examine the situation

$$
\begin{array}{l}
1: xyzw \\
2: xyzw \\
3: yzwx \\
4: zwyx \\
5: wyzx.
\end{array}
$$

show that although x is the plurality winner from {x, y, z, w}, it loses under a simple majority vote comparison with *every* other alternative.

84. The *Kramer score*, K(y), of alternative y at profile u is the *smallest* value of $N(xP_iy)$ over all alternatives x different from y. The *Kramer Rule*

selects from a set v of alternatives the set $C_u(v)$ of those alternatives with largest Kramer score.

a. At profile u given by

$$1: xy(zw)$$
$$2: yzxw$$
$$3: wzyx$$
$$4: (xyz)w$$
$$5: ywxz$$

confirm the Kramer scores as $K(x)=2$; $K(y)=1$; $K(z)=3$; $K(w)=3$.

b. Show that if at u, xP_iy for all i, then $x \in v$ implies $y \notin C_u(v)$.

c. Show that if there is a Condorcet winner in v at u then the Kramer rule selects exactly the set of Condorcet winners.

We have now seen several modifications of simple majority voting designed to deal with occasions when more than two alternatives are available; they each have some significant problems. But equally important, they give very different results from each other. While each embodies some of our notions of democracy and fairness, they may yield different choices at the same situation. To illustrate, consider the 10 individual situation

$$1\&2: ywxz$$
$$3\&4: yxzw$$
$$5\&6: xzwy$$
$$7: zxyw$$
$$8: zwxy$$
$$9\&10: wxzy.$$

The plurality winner is y; with initial arbitrary ordering wxyz, the staging procedure gives z while the Condorcet winner is x.

The inescapable inference is that social choice depends as much on methods of aggregation (that is, on social institutions) as it does on individual values and tastes.[1]

In the next chapter we will more carefully and formally describe both individual tastes and methods of aggregation.

Further Reading

For more discussion of these and other extensions of majority voting, read *Voting Procedures* (Oxford University Press, 1984) by Michael Dummett an Oxford philosopher who writes on the Italian philosopher-mathematician Frege and even on tarot!

---

[1] Riker, William H., *Liberalism Against Populism* (W. H. Freeman; San Francisco, 1982) p. 91.

Chapter 6. Social Choice Rules

In this chapter we are going to start fresh. Now that we have reasons to look beyond simple majority voting, we want to explore a range of possible social choice procedures. We must reintroduce a lot of earlier ideas in a broader context of general social choice rules. We are going to be very precise and very formal. Partly we are doing this because some of the ideas are both subtle and slippery and can not be well conveyed just by examples and hand waving but require precise definition. But more important is preparation for Chapters like 7, 8 and 10 where we are going to prove impossibility theorems. Impossibility theorems tell us there are *no* social choice rules satisfying a certain list of appealing criteria. Now it is usually easy to show that a given social choice rule satisfies a list of clear criteria or fails to satisfy it. But to prove *no* rule satisfies such a list, you must work with all logically possible social choice rules and you can't even make a beginning on that unless you have a clear, precise, rigorous notion of what a social choice rule is. Our theorem goal forces us to be rather formal.

Let X be a nonempty set; the elements of X will be called *alternatives*. This language is deliberately neutral. If we are trying to choose office holders, alternatives would be potential candidates for office; if we are studying law making, alternatives would be potential legislative proposals; if we are studying income distribution, alternatives would be vectors (lists) of numbers of income levels (one number for each individual). At an extreme – but an extreme sometimes useful to think about – alternatives would be complete descriptions of potential consumption, production, exchange and inventory situations for all agents in an economy possibly including a description of all interpersonal relationships and both public and private behavior. The elements of X must only be mutually incompatible. If one alternative finally prevails and is selected, no other alternative can also prevail.

Sometimes when choices have to be made, not all conceivable alternatives are currently available. Some logically possible candidates for office may not be legally of age or of residence; they may be institutionalized; they may be able to declare themselves out of the running. Not all logically possible legislative proposals may be brought before us; for example, legislative rules may require that for two proposals to be currently admissible they must exhibit some minimal difference of degree: we won't separately consider two budgets that differ from one another by one penny for one project. A nonempty subset of X, labeled v, to be interpreted as the set of alternatives that are currently available, is called an *agenda*.

What information will we draw on as a basis for our choice from an agenda? We start by working with the same kind of information used by the voting rules we discussed in the previous chapters: the preferences of individuals over the alternatives. Let N be the set of individuals. There are lots of difficulties we are still going to skip over regarding the determination of N. How do we determine who is a member of the club, who gets selected to the legislature, who enjoys citizenship? How do we judge choices made on the basis of preferences of members of N when those choices affect people outside N: aliens, citizens of other countries, the unborn? Important matters, but this book has nothing to add on them. So that we can simplify our notation, we will assume individuals have numeric labels: 1, 2, ..., n, rather than more complicated labels like Carl Friedrich Gauss or Agatha Christie. Because we are now fixing the size of N, we will not be considering further in this text the criterion of Chapter 5 that was concerned with consistency under changes in constituencies.

Let i be an individual in N. With each i we associate a *preference relation*, R_i, on X.[1] If x and y are alternatives, we read xR_iy as "individual i determines alternative x to be at least as good as alternative y" or "i weakly prefers x to y." There are three properties that each R_i will be assumed to satisfy throughout this book.

1) R_i is reflexive: xR_ix for all $x \in X$.

This is pretty innocuous and is really just an agreement on language rather than a description of behavior or an assumed constraint on behavior. Everyone finds an alternative to be "at least as good as" itself, no matter what the alternative is.

2) R_i is complete: xR_iy or yR_ix (or both) for all $x, y \in X$.

If x and y are identical, this is already taken care of by reflexivity; completeness has new content when x and y are different. Given any two distinct alternatives, either the first is at least as good as the second or the second is at least as good as the first. It does not mean one is strictly better than the other; i may be indifferent between the two. But a comparison *can* be made. This is certainly *not* an innocuous assumption. I conceivably could ask you to judge between two alternatives so unlike one another you just can't compare them. Maybe x is an ascetic life capped by a Nobel Prize and universal acclaim while y is life on an otherwise deserted island with "nothing but" plentiful food, shelter and the mate of your choice. It's certainly possible to imagine someone simply unable to express a comparison between these. Such a possibility is assumed away here.

Because we assume completeness there are exactly three possibilities for each pair x, y of alternatives:

    a) xR_iy and *not* yR_ix; we then say "i strictly prefers x to y" or "i strongly prefers x to y" and write xP_iy.

    b) yR_ix and *not* xR_iy; then yP_ix, i.e., i strongly prefers y to x.

    c) xR_iy and also yR_ix; we then say "i is indifferent between x and y" and write xI_iy.

Notice that reflexivity implies xI_ix for all $x \in X$. Also it should be clear that xI_iy if and only if yI_ix.

---

[1] We treat preference as a subjective phenomenon; it must connect with an individual. This text will not discuss "society's preferences," a phrase deemed quite misleading here.

3) R_i is transitive: For all x, y, z $\in$ X, if both xR_iy and yR_iz, then xR_iz.

Transitivity is often described as a requirement of *consistency*. If you like x at least as well as y and like y at least as well as z, it seems consistent to also like x at least as well as z. Especially would we think i a little strange if he were to say he strongly prefers x to y and strongly prefers y to z but doesn't find x to be at least as good as z. But more controversial conclusions flow from transitivity; the following exercises will lead us to one version of controversy.

Exercises.

In each of Exercises 85 to 89, suppose R_i is transitive and prove the property claimed.

85. For all x_1, x_2, ..., x_m in X, if

$$x_1R_ix_2 \text{ and } x_2R_ix_3 \text{ and } ... \text{ and } x_{m-1}R_ix_m$$

then

$$x_1R_ix_m.$$

86. For all x, y, z in X, if xR_iy and yP_iz, then xP_iz. (In particular, xP_iy and yP_iz imply xP_iz.)
87. For all x, y, z in X, xP_iy and yR_iz together imply xP_iz.
88. For all x, y, z, if xI_iy and yI_iz, then xI_iz.
89. For all x_1, x_2, ..., x_m in X if

$$x_1I_ix_2 \text{ and } x_2I_ix_3 \text{ and } ... \text{ and } x_{m-1}I_ix_m,$$

then

$$x_1I_ix_m.$$

Exercise 88 tells us I_i is transitive when R_i is. But suppose indifference arises because of threshold effects; xI_iy only because x and y are not sufficiently different for us to notice. For example, suppose we have a large collection of alternatives x_0, x_1, x_2, x_3, ... where x_j means a cup of tea with j grains of sugar in it. The difference between x_j and x_{j+1} may be below some threshold of perception and it may then be that our individual i will have $x_jI_ix_{j+1}$ for all j. But then Exercise 89 tells us

$$x_0I_ix_{1,\,000,\,000,\,000};$$

that i must be indifferent between tea with no sugar in it or tea buried under a billion grains. Not very plausible.

Exercise.

90. Suppose R_i satisfies the following two conditions for all x, y and z:

i.) xP_iy and yP_iz imply xP_iz;
ii.) xP_iy and yI_iz imply xP_iz.

Show that then R_i must be transitive so that also I_i must be transitive.

The conceivable violations of completeness and transitivity suggest that our assumptions lead us to a very shallow and naive psychology. This would be a problem if we wanted to promote a particular social choice procedure – for then we might be vulnerable to the criticism that the procedure works well when applied to "simple" people but might not work well for more complex real people. But we are aiming toward an impossibility theorem. It seems especially dramatic to show that "good" preference aggregation can't take place even when people have simple preferences – for then how much more difficult it would be when individuals' behavior were more complex.

It is these assumptions on R_i that allow us to adopt our simplified notation for preferences: for strict preferences we use left-to-right and for indifference we use parentheses so that

$$i: (xz)y$$

means xI_iz, xP_iy and zP_iy.

Exercises.
91. Show that there are 13 different preference relations on three alternatives and that six of these are strong, i.e., have no indifferences except the trivial indifferences forced by reflexivity.
92. Show that there are 75 different preference relations on four alternatives and that 24 of these are strong.
93. Show that there are $m! = m \cdot (m-1) \cdot (m-2)...3 \cdot 2 \cdot 1$ different strong preference relations on m alternatives.

A *profile* is an assignment of one preference relation to each individual. A profile is what in earlier chapters we called a "situation". Let's count profiles.

Exercises.
94. With just two alternatives, how many different profiles are there if there are four individuals? If there are n individuals?
95. How many profiles are there with three alternatives and three individuals?

To illustrate one more time, suppose there are five individuals and four alternatives. By Exercise 92, there are 75 different preference relations on four alternatives. So as we try to describe a profile, there are 75 possible assignments of preferences to individual 1 and for each of these 75 possible assignments to individual 2 and so on through individual 5. There are thus

$$75 \cdot 75 \cdot 75 \cdot 75 \cdot 75 \approx 2, 373, 000, 000$$

possible profiles.

At a profile, a preference aggregator will direct choices. What choices are made will depend in part on the agenda, the set of admissible alternatives. Given agenda v, we write $C(v)$ for the elements chosen from v by choice function C. We impose two definitional requirements on C: for every v in the domain of C,

$$(i) \ C(v) \subset v;$$
$$(ii) \ C(v) \text{ is not empty.}$$

The second requirement may seem to be just an agreement about language. If we had a first sense of the word "choice" such that not-choosing is an option, we would expand our idea of "agenda" so that it always includes as one alternative the status-quo state, x_0, that results from not-choosing in that first sense. Then with $x_0 \in v$, we have a second sense of "choice" such that $C(v) = \{x_0\} \subset v$ if first sense not-choosing occurs. We will return to this idea right after we introduce the standard domain constraint a few pages from here.

Notice that we do not definitionally require that $C(v)$ be a singleton. $C(v)$ "narrows" the choice down to some subset of v but may have more than one element. Having $C(v)$ a singleton may be desirable and a "good" preference aggregator may generate C's having singleton outcomes, but that will be treated only as one possibly desirable property and not a definitionally required one. Allowing $C(v)$ to be larger than a singleton is tied up with the issue of the informational base for social choice. Suppose the only information we have are preference rankings of individuals and that we are currently looking at the profile in which everyone is indifferent among all alternatives. On what grounds can we narrow $C(v)$ to less than all of v? Either we need some default rule that chooses independently of preferences or we must gather more information to break ties.

We have adopted a notation suggesting C is a function that is to operate on varying agendas. The idea is that we might not know in advance what agenda we are confronting and we may want C to be able to deal with a variety of agendas. The less we know ahead of time about what alternatives will be feasible, the more flexibility we must insist C have by requiring a larger domain of possible v's. We will now show that enlarging the domain of admissible agendas allows greater variation and increases the possible number of choice functions.

Exercises.

Suppose in the following $X = \{x, y, z, w\}$.

96. Suppose the only agenda in the domain of C is $v = X$. Show there are 15 possible different choice functions.

97. Suppose C has in its domain exactly the agendas of size three or four. Show there are $15 \cdot 7 \cdot 7 \cdot 7 \cdot 7 = 36,015$ different possible choice functions.

98. Suppose C has in its domain all nonempty agendas. Show there are $15 \cdot 7 \cdot 7 \cdot 7 \cdot 7 \cdot 3 \cdot 3 \cdot 3 \cdot 3 \cdot 3 \cdot 3 = 26,255,000$ different choice functions.

A *social choice rule* assigns to each of a collection of profiles a corresponding choice function. Just as we don't know what agenda a choice function will face

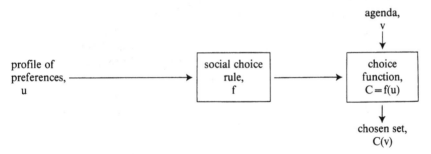

and so will usually require it to be flexible enough to deal with many agendas, we also don't know what profile a social choice rule will have to act on and so we will usually require such a rule to be able to deal with many profiles. Often, indeed, we will ask a social choice rule to have in its domain all logically possible profiles and to assign, at each profile a choice rule that has as domain all logically possible non-empty finite agendas. How many such social choice rules are there? Let's examine a relatively simple case with just five individuals and four alternatives. As we have seen, there are $75 \cdot 75 \cdot 75 \cdot 75 \cdot 75$ possible profiles of preference rankings on four alternatives. At each profile, there are $15 \cdot 7 \cdot 7 \cdot 7 \cdot 7 \cdot 3 \cdot 3 \cdot 3 \cdot 3 \cdot 3 \cdot 3$ different choice functions that could be assigned. Hence the number of possible social choice rules is

$$(15 \cdot 7^4 \cdot 3^6)^{(75^5)} \quad .$$

This number is approximately $10^{235, 000, 000, 000}$, that is, 1, 000, 000, 000, 000, 000, 000, 000, 000, ..., 000, 000, 000, 000, 000, 000, 000, 000, 000 where the ..... shows *some* 0's are missing – we need 235 *billion* 0's here.

The first observation we make about this number is that it is larger than 1. That means there is at least some freedom in selecting a social choice rule. It's that freedom that gives rise to the central part of our subject: the comparative study of social choice rules done with an eye toward helping select "good" rules.

The second observation, of course, is that this number

$$10^{235, 000, 000, 000}$$

is large. Large beyond understanding. By comparison, one recent estimate of the number of seconds in the history of the universe since the big bang is about 10^{19}; the number of protons in the universe is about 10^{79}. If every second we could "record" one of these social choice rules on a proton, there would not have been time enough or space enough to have done but the most infinitesimal fraction of the whole job.

Worse, this number will grow extraordinarily rapidly with the number of alternatives and even more rapidly with the number of individuals. What must it be for a group as large as the U. S. Senate (100 individuals) and for an issue of moderate complexity, say of a dozen alternatives?

The first consequence of the size of this number is that we obviously can *not* do a comparative analysis of social choice rules by going through them one by one; we must examine (large) classes of them. We will usually be looking at classes of rules that satisfy some set of properties we think "desirable".

The second consequence is that, with such an incredibly large number of rules to draw from, we gain the expectation that it will be easy to find "good" one. That is, if we were to write down even a long list of "desirable" properties, we anticipate being able to find one, or many, even a huge number of rules satisfying all these properties. It is this expectation that provides the drama of the impossibility theorems. We will look at very short lists of three to five seemingly desirable properties and find that *none* of the $10^{235, 000, 000, 000}$ rules satisfy those few properties.

Let's start to look at examples. To describe a social choice rule we need to see what choice function C_u the rule selects when it faces profile $u = (R_1, R_2, ..., R_n)$.

Example 1. $C_u(v) = v$ for all profiles u and all agendas v. This rule is totally insensitive to individual preferences since it assigns the same choice function to every profile. (Of course, because of this it might satisfy some egalitarian criterion of equal treatment of individuals, but only in a trivial way.) Worse, the choice function assigned is *useless*; C_u never does any narrowing at all from any agenda of available alternatives.

Example 2. Suppose X can be listed: $X = \{x_1, x_2, x_3, ...\}$ possibly but not necessarily finite. At each profile u, our second rule selects the choice function C* which selects from an agenda v the earliest listed element in v:

$$C^*(v) = \{x_i\} \text{ where } x_i \in v \text{ and } i \leq j \text{ for all } j \text{ such}$$
$$\text{that } x_j \in v.$$

This rule does vastly better than the first at narrowing agendas; each v is reduced by C* to a singleton. But like Example 1, it does badly with respect to basing choices on individual preferences; all preferences are ignored. (For that reason, it again treats individuals equally.)

We can use these two examples to illustrate properties that will play a huge role in the rest of this book. First, both rules "work" everywhere. By that I mean that each rule is defined at every profile and yields a choice function that works at every agenda. The domain of each rule is all logically possible profiles and at each such profile there is selected a choice function with the set of all logically possible agendas as domain. This, in an extreme form, is the flexibility requirement we raised earlier. For most purposes, we can relax this requirement slightly by only insisting that all *finite* agendas be in the domain of each choice function. If we add conditions on the numbers of individuals and alternatives, we get the *standard domain constraint*:

> i) there are at least three alternatives in X;
> ii) there are at least three individuals in N;
> iii) the social choice rule has as domain all logically
> possible profiles of preference orderings on X;
> iv) each choice function that is an output of the rule
> has in its domain all finite nonempty agendas.

Both Example 1 and Example 2 satisfy the standard domain constraint.

Notice that part iv) of this constraint prevents us from interpreting agendas as always containing a 'status-quo' alternative, x_0. Part iv) requires C to work at finite agendas that exclude x_0.

A second common aspect of these examples is their insensitivity to individual preferences. So we next introduce properties that will require some sensitivity. In fact we will require more than just that C_u must not be invariant with respect to u; we want C_u to respond "positively" to preferences. If $v = \{x, y\}$ and at profile $u = (R_1, R_2, ..., R_n)$ we have xP_iy for all i, while at profile $u' = (R_1', R_2', ..., R_n')$ we have $yP_i'x$ for all i, we not only want

$$C_u(v) \neq C_{u'}(v)$$

we want particularly

$$C_u(v)=\{x\} \text{ and } C_{u'}(v)=\{y\}.$$

At u, why choose y from v when v contains an alternative x that *everyone* strictly prefers to y?

Now so far we have described a sensitivity requirement only when the agenda consists of two alternatives. This gets generalized in the *weak Pareto condition:*

> Let the social choice rule select choice function C_u at profile u. Suppose at u everyone unanimously strictly prefers one alternative, say x, to another, say y; then if x is available (i.e., $x \in v$), y won't be chosen (i.e., $y \notin C_u(v)$).

This doesn't mean x will be chosen (maybe there's something else, z, in v that everyone prefers to x), only that y won't be chosen. Often we will require the somewhat more stringent *strong Pareto condition:*

> Let the social choice rule select choice function C_u at profile u. Suppose at u everyone unanimously finds one alternative, x, to be at least as good as another, y, and at least one individual strictly prefers x to y. Then if x is available $(x \in v)$, y won't be chosen $(y \notin C_u(v))$.

This condition is "strong" in the sense that it kicks more alternatives in v out of $C_u(v)$ than does the weak Pareto condition. If everyone considers x to be at least as good as y and *some but not all* are indifferent between x and y, then if x is in v, the strong condition forces y out of $C_u(v)$ but the weak condition doesn't.

Both Example 1 and Example 2 violate even the weak Pareto condition. The Example 1 rule yields choice functions that never kick any alternatives out of $C_u(v)$. Example 2 is a bit different. If $i < j$ and everybody prefers x_i to x_j, then if x_i is available x_j won't be chosen. But x_j's exclusion from $C_u(v)$ isn't due to the universal preference for x_i; it is due simply to $i < j$ and x_i being in v. When $i > j$, then even if everyone strictly prefers x_i to x_j and $x_i \in v$, you won't be able to say x_j is excluded; x_j will be in $C_u(v)$ if and only if x_j is the lowest indexed alternative in v.

Let's construct a social choice rule that does satisfy a Pareto condition. Define a new relation among alternatives as follows: x is *Pareto-superior* to y at profile $u=(R_1, R_2, ..., R_n)$ if

> i) xR_iy for all individuals i in N;
> ii) xP_iy for at least one individual i in N.

Exercises.
  99. If x is Pareto-superior to y, then y is not Pareto-superior to x.
  100. If x is Pareto-superior to y and y is Pareto-superior to z, then x is Pareto-superior to z.

We use this to construct

Example 3. $C_u(v) = \{x \ / \ x \in v$ and if $y \in v$ with $y \neq x$ then x is Pareto-superior to $y\}$.

This choice rule selects from v those alternatives that are Pareto-superior to all others in v. This rule not only satisfies our sensitivity condition, it does substantial narrowing.

Exercises.

101. Show that the social choice rule of Example 3 satisfies the strong Pareto condition.

102. Show that for the social choice rule of Example 3, if C_u exists then each $C_u(v)$ is a singleton.

The phrasing of Exercise 102 is carefully chosen. It does not say (as we said of Example 2) that at every u there is a singleton $C_u(v)$. The distinction is that sometimes the C_u of Example 3 doesn't exist. Remember that it was part of the definition of a choice function that it must always select a *nonempty* subset of an agenda. Suppose there are three individuals, $N = \{1, 2, 3\}$, and three alternatives, $X = \{x, y, z\}$ and consider the profile given by

$$1: x(yz)$$
$$2: y(xz)$$
$$3: z(xy).$$

Then if $v = X$ there is no alternative that is Pareto-superior to all the others; in fact no alternative is Pareto-superior to *any* of the others. The procedure used in the definition of Example 3 yields an empty set at this profile and agenda. This rule violates the standard domain constraint.

Accordingly, we will modify the idea behind the construction of Example 3 so as to satisfy both the standard domain constraint and the strong Pareto condition.

Example 4. $C_u(v) = \{x \ / \ x \in v$ and there does not exist a $y \in v$ such that y is Pareto-superior to $x\}$.

This example is both flexible and sensitive to preferences.

Exercises.

103. a. Determine the choice function generated by the rule of Example 4 at the profile u:

$$1: xyzw$$
$$2: xwyz$$
$$3: yxwz$$
$$4: yzxw$$

b. Show that the social choice rule of Example 4 satisfies the strong Pareto condition.

104. Show that the social choice rule of Example 4 satisfies the standard domain constraint. What you must show is that for every u and every finite v the set described is not empty.

Alternatives for which there are no available Pareto-superior alternatives are called *Pareto optimal*. Clearly, the rule of Example 4 that selects at each profile the choice function that picks out the Pareto optimals treats everyone equally. It has in common with Example 1 an equal treatment of alternatives (in contrast with Example 2 which treats lower indexed alternatives very differently from higher indexed alternatives).

A principle drawback to this rule is that it often does very little narrowing. There are often *lots* of Pareto optimal alternatives in v. To illustrate how this happens, suppose there are millions of individuals and we examine a profile where all but one of them have the same strong ordering:

$$xyz...m$$

and the one other individual has the exact opposite ordering

$$m...zyx;$$

then for this rule $C_u(v) = v$ for all agendas v.

The reason very little narrowing occurs is that this rule confers upon everyone a great deal of *inclusionary* power. To see this, note that if any individual has at profile u a single alternative at the top of his ordering (i.e., that alternative is strictly preferred to all others), then with this rule, that alternative must be among those chosen from any agenda in which it occurs. To describe this, we say individual i is a *weak dictator*[2] if for every pair of alternatives, x and y, every profile $u = (R_1, R_2, ..., R_n)$ and every agenda v, if xP_iy then

$$y \in C_u(v) \text{ implies } x \in C_u(v).$$

The adjective "weak" in this definition refers to the *inclusionary* nature of i's power. We shall discuss exclusionary power after three Exercises.

Exercises.
105. Show that in the social choice rules of Examples 1, 3 and 4, *everyone* is a weak dictator. *That's* why so little narrowing occurs there.
106. Show that in the social choice rule of Example 2, *no one* is a weak dictator.
107. Show that if a social choice rule satisfies the standard domain constraint and i is a weak dictator, then if at u xP_iy we must have

$$x \in C_u(\{x, y\}).$$

Conferring *inclusionary* power on individuals or small groups of individuals prevents narrowing; it makes the choice functions less effective. Conferring *exclusionary* power on individuals or small groups is much stronger and conflicts much

---

[2] Again, the reader is to be warned away from the possible confusion that might result from the use here as a technical term of a word like "dictator" that in natural language has a quite different as well as much richer meaning.

more directly with our most strongly held views on the appropriate distribution of power, i.e., with our political philosophy.

A subset S of the set N of all individuals is called a *coalition*. For a social choice rule that maps u to C_u, a coalition S is called *decisive for alternative x against alternative y* if at every single profile in the domain of the rule where everyone in S finds x to be at least as good as y and at least one individual in S strictly prefers x to y, then at every agenda v containing x, y won't be chosen. If for every pair of alternatives x and y in X the coalition S is decisive for x against y, then we simply say S is *decisive*. The strong Pareto condition is the requirement that the set N of all individuals is decisive. While we may be willing to endow a large coalition like N with the exclusionary power of decisiveness, we are normally much less happy with such power residing in a small group. At an extreme, if a decisive coalition consists of a single individual, $S = \{i\}$, we say i is a *dictator*. If i is a dictator, then $C_u(v)$ will just be the element of v most preferred by i at u among the alternatives of v if there is such a unique most preferred element. If, at u, i is indifferent among some elements of v but prefers all these to the other elements of v, i's dictatorship ensures that $C_u(v)$ will be some subset of that topmost set of i's. Thus, if i is a dictator, the preferences of other individuals can only play the role of breaking ties within i's topmost indifference set.

Exercises.

108. Show that in Example 1, no coalition is decisive for any one alternative against another.
109. Show that in Example 2 every coalition (even ø!) is decisive for x_0 against x_1 but no coalition is decisive for x_1 against x_0.
110. Show that in Example 4 no *proper* subset of N is decisive for any one alternative against another.
111. Suppose S is decisive for x against y and $S \subset S' \subset N$. Does that imply that S' is also decisive for x against y?
112. If a social choice rule satisfies the standard domain constraint; then N can not contain two disjoint decisive sets. In particular, if a rule has a dictator, it has just one.
113. Can a rule have a dictator and someone *else* who is a weak dictator?
114. Every dictator is a weak dictator but a weak dictator need not be a dictator.
115. Prove: If a rule has a dictator then the weak Pareto condition must be satisfied.
116. Can the same be said about the strong Pareto condition?

Exercise 112 indicates an interrelationship between decisive sets and domain constraints. Domain constraints also influence how we feel about the distribution of decisiveness power. Suppose that we know there will always be unanimity. Everyone will always have the same preference as everyone else; the "will of the people" will always be unambiguous. Then we need only design a social choice rule for profiles $u = (R_1, R_2, ..., R_n)$ such that

$$R_i = R_j$$

for all i, j in N. Endowing a small group, even a single individual, in these circumstances with the power of being a decisive set seems vastly less offensive than making say {1} decisive when the only admissible profiles have #1's preferences the opposite of the ordering held unanimously by everyone else.

Now let's return to the Condorcet winner extension of majority voting. Remember that $N(xR_iy)$ is the number of individuals $i \in N$ for whom xR_iy at profile $u = (R_1, R_2, ..., R_n)$.

Example 5. $C_u(v) = \{x \in v \ / \ N(xR_iy) \geq N(yR_ix)$ for all $y \in v\}$.

Exercises.

117. Use the voting paradox profile to show that with exactly three individuals the standard domain constraint is not satisfied by the rule of Example 5.
118. Use Exercise 117 to show that with *more than* three individuals, the standard domain constraint is not satisfied by the rule of Example 5.
119. For this rule, what sets of individuals are decisive? In particular, is there a dictator and is the strong Pareto condition satisfied?

This example shares with Example 3 a failure of the standard domain constraint. We modified Example 3 to Example 4 by giving up on asking chosen alternatives to be Pareto superior to all others and only asking that no available alternative be Pareto superior to any chosen alternative. This is a meaningful modification only because "Pareto superior" is an *incomplete* relation, i.e., sometimes neither "x is Pareto superior to y" nor "y is Pareto superior to x" is true. In Example 5, however, for all x and y either

$$N(xR_iy) \geq N(yR_ix) \ or \ N(yR_ix) \geq N(xR_iy).$$

So, if we tried to define a modified rule to avoid empty chosen sets by the formula

$$C_u(v) = \{x \ / \ x \in v \text{ and there does not exist a } y \in v$$
$$\text{such that } N(yR_ix) > N(xR_iy)\}$$

we simply get Example 5 back again. It will take a quite different kind of modification to get rid of the empty chosen sets. Two such modifications are found in the next few examples.

Example 6. $C_u(v) = \{x \ / \text{ for each } y \in v, \text{ there are alternatives } y_1, y_2, ..., y_t \text{ in X}$ such that $N(xR_iy_1) \geq N(y_1R_ix), N(y_1R_iy_2) \geq N(y_2R_iy_1), ..., N(y_tR_iy) \geq N(yR_iy_t)\}$.

This rule has x in agenda v chosen just when it bests every other alternative y in v either *directly* by straight comparison under simple majority voting:

$$N(xR_iy) \geq N(yR_ix)$$

or *indirectly* by beating under simple majority vote some third alternative y_1 that in turn beats y:

$$N(xR_iy_1) \geq N(y_1R_ix) \ and \ N(y_1R_iy) \geq N(yR_iy_1)$$

or more indirectly still by beating under simple majority vote an alternative y_1 that beats an alternative y_2 that in turn beats y and so on.

Let's see what this rule does at the voting paradox profile u that is not in the domain of the rule of Exercise 5:

$$1: xyz$$
$$2: yzx$$
$$3: zxy.$$

If $v = \{x, y, z\}$, then $C_u(v)$ will include x because x beats y directly

$$N(xR_iy) = 2 > 1 = N(yR_ix)$$

and beats z indirectly since y beats z directly

$$N(yR_iz) = 2 > 1 = N(zR_iy).$$

By symmetry, y and z are also in $C(v)$ which must then be all of v.

Exercises.
120. If a beats b indirectly and b beats c indirectly, then a beats c indirectly.
121. Show that this rule *does* satisfy the standard domain constraint.
122. Show that this rule does not have a dictator.

As this voting paradox profile calculation suggests, this rule may cause too little narrowing. We have seen that insufficient narrowing may be caused by too few decisive sets. Here if there are more alternatives than voters not even the coalition N of all individuals is decisive, i.e., the strong Pareto condition fails. In fact, even the weak Pareto condition fails. To see this, consider the profile u':

$$1: xyzw$$
$$2: yzwx$$
$$3: zwxy.$$

At u', z is Pareto-superior to w, in fact, everyone strongly prefers z to w. If the weak Pareto condition held, we would have $w \notin C_{u'}(\{wxyz\})$. But:

  (i) w beats x directly;
  (ii) w beats y indirectly because x beats y directly;
  (iii) w beats z indirectly because y beats z directly.

Exercise.
123. Show that for this rule no coalition is decisive.

Example 7. $C_u(v) = \{x \in v \, / \, \text{for each } y \in v \text{ there are alternatives } y_1, y_2, ..., y_t \text{ in } v \text{ such that } N(xR_iy_1) \geq N(y_1R_iy), N(y_1R_iy_2) \geq N(y_2R_iy_1), ..., N(y_tR_iy) \geq N(yR_iy_t)\}$.

This rule differs from Example 6 in that the sequence of alternatives that establish x beating y indirectly here must all be from v whereas in Example 6 we could use alternatives from X that were outside v. Because our discussion of Example 6 always treated the case $v = X$, nothing we have seen so far allows us to see the distinction between Examples 6 and 7; we will have to see that distinction on agen-

das of less than all of X. To facilitate this comparison, we will adopt a slight variation in notation: the rule in Example 6 will assign to profile u the choice function
C_u^6 while the rule in Example 7 will assign choice function C_u^7. Now consider the
voting paradox profile, u, again:

$$1: xyz$$
$$2: yzx$$
$$3: zxy.$$

Lets look this time at the agenda $v = \{x, y\}$. Since x beats y directly under simple
majority voting, we will have $x \in C_u^6(v)$ and $x \in C_u^7(v)$. Example 7 would have
$C_u^7(v) = \{x\}$; because v has just two alternatives, there is no way y can indirectly
beat x through alternatives *in* v. But in Example 6 we can build a sequence
through z; y beats z directly and z beats x directly, so y beats x indirectly. So
$C_u^6(v) = \{x, y\}$.

Exercises.
124. Show that the rule of Example 7 satisfies the standard domain
constraint.
125. Show that for the rule of Example 7 no coalition is decisive; in
particular there is no dictator and the strong Pareto condition fails.
There is however a *pairwise* strong Pareto condition: for all profiles u
and all pairs x, y of alternatives, if at u, xR_iy for all i and xP_i for at least
one i, then $C_u(\{x, y\}) = \{x\}$.
126. Show that this rule also fails the weak Pareto condition.

We will reconsider Examples 6 and 7 after we have described the Borda rules
in Examples 9 and 10. But first we look at a different way of modifying the majority vote procedure in Example 5 to eliminate its failure at some profiles and agendas to yield nonempty chosen sets. This different way is a more formal version of
the staging approach studied in Chapter 5.

Example 8. In this example we are going to suppose that the set X of all alternatives can be labeled by the integers:

$$X = \{x_1, x_2, x_3, \ldots\}.$$

While in Examples 6 and 7 we used majority vote comparisons between all possible pairs of distinct alternatives, here many fewer comparisons will be carried out.
At each agenda of $m+1$ alternatives, a sequence of only m voting comparisons
will take place. Let $v = \{x_{v0}, x_{v1}, \ldots, x_{vm}\}$ where $v0 < v1 < \ldots < vm$. The first voting comparison is between x_{v0} and x_{v1}. The winner w_1 will be x_{v0} if x_{v0} beats x_{v1}; it
will be x_{v1} if x_{v1} beats x_{v0}. This rule always uses a tie breaking method which fa-
vors the lower labeled alternative (x_{v0} at this first stage).

$$w_1 = \begin{cases} x_{v0} \text{ if } N(x_{v0}R_ix_{v1}) \geq N(x_{v1}R_ix_{v0}) \\ \\ x_{v1} \text{ if } N(x_{v1}R_ix_{v0}) > N(x_{v0}R_ix_{v1}). \end{cases}$$

At the second stage, w_1, the winner of the first stage, is pitted against x_{v2} by simple majority voting to determine the second stage winner, w_2:

$$w_2 = \begin{cases} w_1 \text{ if } N(w_1 R_i x_{v2}) \geq N(x_{v2} R_i w_1) \\ x_{v2} \text{ if } N(x_{v2} R_i w_1) > N(w_1 R_i x_{v2}). \end{cases}$$

After t stages have been completed in this fashion, we define w_{t+1}, the winner of the next or $t+1^{st}$ stage, by

$$w_{t+1} = \begin{cases} w_t \text{ if } N(w_t R_i x_{t+1}) \geq N(x_{t+1} R_i w_t) \\ x_{t+1} \text{ if } N(x_{t+1} R_i w_t) > N(w_t R_i x_{t+1}). \end{cases}$$

The winner w_m at the mth or last stage is the element chosen:

$$C_u(v) = \{w_m\}.$$

Exercises.

127. Show that this rule satisfies the standard domain constraint.
128. What sets are decisive for x_1 against x_2? For x_2 against x_1?
129. What sets are decisive? Is the strong Pareto condition satisfied? The weak Pareto condition?
130. Does this rule have a dictator? A weak dictator?

As we have seen in Chapter 5, part of what makes this rule interesting is its vulnerability to two kinds of strategic manipulation. The outcome may be altered by the agent who orders the stages and it may be altered by individuals who have a self interest in sending false messages to the rule. Not only are manipulable rules wasteful of resources that go into manipulation activity, they are less likely to possess "legitimacy." More will be said about agenda manipulation when we get to the subject of "explicability" later in this chapter and more will be said about sending false preference information in Chapter 10 on "strategy-proofness." Now we turn to the first of the Borda rules.

Example 9. Assume again that X is finite. Then associated with any preference ordering R_i there is a ranking function r_i that associates an integer with each alternative: $r_i(x)$ is the number of alternatives strictly preferred to x. Given a profile $u = (R_1, R_2, ..., R_n)$, there is a ranking function r given by

$$r(x) = \sum_i r_i(x).^3$$

This ranking function is the main ingredient in the *global Borda rule*:

$$C_u(v) = \{x \; / \; r(x) \leq r(y) \text{ for all } y \in v\}.$$

---

[3] This ranking computation is a purely formal operation on ordinal comparisons and should *not* be interpreted as a *cardinal* "utility."

The value of r(x) is called the *Borda count* of x and this rule has us choose from v those alternatives with minimal Borda count.

To illustrate this rule, consider the profile u:

$$1: xyzw$$
$$2: yzwx$$
$$3: zwxy.$$

First we calculate the ranking functions:

alt.	r_1	r_2	r_3	$r = \sum r_i$
x	0	3	2	5
y	1	0	3	4
z	2	1	0	3
w	3	2	1	6.

So at this profile u we would have, for example, $C_u(\{xyzw\}) = \{z\}$, $C_u(\{xyw\}) = \{y\}$.

Exercises.
131. Show that this rule satisfies the standard domain constraint.
132. Show that this rule has no dictator or weak dictator.
133. Show that this rule satisfies the strong Pareto condition.
134. Show that with three individuals and four alternatives no coalition of less than all individuals is decisive.

We will now use this rule to illustrate a new property of social choice rules. At profile u above, we saw $C_u(\{xyw\}) = \{y\}$. Keep this in mind while we examine a second profile u':

$$1: xzyw$$
$$2: ywxz$$
$$3: wxzy$$

with ranking functions

alt.	r_1	r_2	r_3	$r = \sum r_i$
x	0	2	1	3
y	2	0	3	5
z	1	3	2	6
w	3	1	0	4.

Here we have, for example, $C_{u'}(\{xyw\}) = \{x\}$. What makes this remarkable is that we are getting different choices from this agenda $\{x, y, w\}$ at u and u' although the two profiles *agree completely on this agenda*. To see this agreement, look at each of these two profiles "restricted to $\{x, y, w\}$;" i.e., see what each profile looks like if we erase all alternatives (here just z) not in the agenda, $\{x, y, w\}$. For both profiles we would get the same restricted profile:

$$1: xyw$$
$$2: ywx$$
$$3: wxy.$$

A very famous - and controversial - property of social choice rules is *independence of irrelevant alternatives* which says that this behavior doesn't occur; if two profiles u, u', restricted to an agenda v are identical, then the choices made from that agenda should be the same:

$$C_u(v) = C_{u'}(v).$$

Exercises.

135. Show that Examples 1, 2, 3, 4, 5 and 7 satisfy independence of irrelevant alternatives.

136. Show that Example 6 does *not* satisfy independence of irrelevant alternatives by examining agenda $v = \{x, y\}$ and profiles

$$u: 1: xyz$$
$$2: yzx$$
$$3: zxy$$

and

$$u': 1: xyz$$
$$2: yxz$$
$$3: xyz.$$

Most of the controversy surrounding the property of independence of irrelevant alternatives has stemmed from misunderstanding. For example, many have thought that it is the independence requirement that precludes us from incorporating "intensity" of preference into social choices. But it is a part of our definition of *social choice rule* that C_u's are selected based only on the information in a profile of ordinal preference relations. These simple preference relations *do not contain* intensity information that could be used by social choice rules failing independence.

A first remark to make is that very many of the social choice rules actually adopted in the real world do satisfy independence. In trying to make a choice between alternative candidates that are available in the next presidential election, we must face the fact that Thomas Jefferson is not a feasible choice. Should we consider individuals' preferences between Jefferson and feasible candidates as well as that part of their orderings that deal only with comparing the feasible candidates? Not many real world rules do this. In fact, most rules would only have us submit preferences over a *small* number from among the feasible candidates and not even pay attention to our preferences over *all feasible* candidates much less solicit information about irrelevant (because infeasible) alternatives.

Second, there is a "slippery slope" argument: if we pay attention to preferences not only over feasible candidates but also with respect to Thomas Jefferson, how about Socrates? Buffalo Bill? Fictional people? Animals? Fictional animals? Androids? Rocks? It is costly in terms of resources to gather and process information about preferences - independence is a requirement that we conserve those resources.

Third, there is reason to believe a connection between (i) independence and (ii) vulnerability to strategic misrepresentation. Your vote for feasible x against feasible y may have consequences - you may help to exclude y. If you *really* prefer y to x and so don't want to exclude y you'd better not cast a vote for x against y. But a vote for feasible x against *infeasible* y can *not* exclude y since y can't be chosen any way. Thus you may feel free to vote that way even if you really prefer y to x.

In our next example, we will modify Example 9 in the same way that Example 7 modified Example 6. We will guarantee satisfaction of independence by ranking only within an agenda.

Example 10. Given an agenda v, there is associated with each preference ordering R_i a ranking function r_i^v that associates an integer with each alternative *in v*: $r_i^v(x)$ is the number of alternatives *also in v* that are strictly preferred to x. Given a profile $u = (R_1, R_2, ..., R_n)$, there is for each v a ranking function $r^v(x) = \sum r_i^v(x)$, which we will call the *local Borda count* for x. This allows us to define the *local Borda rule* by

$$C_u(v) = \{x \in v \; / \; r^v(x) \leq r^v(y) \text{ for all } y \in v\}.$$

Consider again the profile

$$u: 1: xyzw$$
$$2: yzwx$$
$$3: zwxy.$$

If $v = X$, then there is no distinction between the choices made by Example 9 and Example 10. Obviously there is also no distinction on agendas of size one.

Exercise.

137. Show that on agendas of size two, this rule agrees with the simple majority vote rule.

Because of Exercise 137 and the remarks preceding it, we know most of the choice function already:

$$C_u(\{x\}) = \{x\}, \; C_u(\{y\}) = \{y\}, \; C_u(\{z\}) = \{z\}, \; C_u(\{w\}) = \{w\},$$
$$C_u(\{x, y\}) = \{x\}, \; C_u(\{x, z\}) = \{z\}, \; C_u(\{x, w\}) = \{w\},$$
$$C_u(\{y, z\}) = \{y\}, \; C_u(\{y, w\}) = \{y\}, \; C_u(\{z, w\}) = \{z\},$$
$$C_u(\{x, y, z, w\}) = \{z\}.$$

It remains to figure out the behavior of C_u on the four agendas of size three.

i) $v = \{x, y, z\}$

	r_1^v	r_2^v	r_3^v	r^v
x	0	2	1	3
y	1	0	2	3
z	2	1	0	3

$C_u(\{x, y, z\}) = \{x, y, z\}.$

ii) $v = \{x, y, w\}$

	r_1^v	r_2^v	r_3^v	r^v
x	0	2	1	3
y	1	0	2	3
w	2	1	0	3

$$C_u(\{x, y, w\}) = \{x, y, w\}.$$

iii) $v = \{x, z, w\}$

	r_1^v	r_2^v	r_3^v	r^v
x	0	2	2	4
z	1	0	0	1
w	2	1	1	4

$$C_u(\{x, z, w\}) = \{z\}.$$

iv) $v = \{y, z, w\}$

	r_1^v	r_2^v	r_3^v	r^v
y	0	0	1	1
z	1	1	2	4
w	2	2	0	4

$$C_u(\{y, z, w\}) = \{y\}.$$

Now that you see how the rule works you should do the next set of exercises to see that this rule satisfies most of the desirable conditions so far described.

Exercises.

138. Show that this rule satisfies the standard domain constraint.
139. Show that this rule satisfies the strong Pareto condition.
140. Show that this rule has no dictator or even weak dictator.
141. Show that this rule satisfies independence of irrelevant alternatives.

One problem with this rule is similar to a manipulation problem of the staging rule we studied back in Example 8. Suppose we decide not to confront the whole agenda at once but to deal with it piecewise by splitting v into parts S and T so

$$v = S \cup T;$$

choose from each part getting $C_u(S)$ and $C_u(T)$, then putting these selections together and choosing from the result, ending up with

$$C_u(C_u(S) \cup C_u(T)).$$

Splitting large issues into parts this way is as common in legislative politics as in electoral politics (where candidates are divided into parties and the choices are made from among the party choices). Now suppose S', T' were a different way of splitting v into sub-agendas

$$v = S' \cup T'.$$

If it were the case that

$$C_u(C_u(S) \cup C_u(T)) \neq C_u(C_u(S') \cup C_u(T'))$$

then it will become in someone's interest to waste resources in agenda manipulation, in seeing that say v is split up as $S \cup T$ rather than $S' \cup T'$.

Recall the staging rule of Example 8; let the alternatives be $\{x_0, x_1, x_2\}$ and consider the voting paradox profile u:

$$1: x_0 x_1 x_2$$
$$2: x_1 x_2 x_0$$
$$3: x_2 x_0 x_1.$$

If $S=\{x_0, x_1\}$ and $T=\{x_2\}$,

$$C_u(C_u(\{x_0, x_1\}) \cup C_u(\{x_2\})) = C_u(\{x_0\} \cup \{x_2\}) = C_u(\{x_0, x_2\}) = \{x_2\}.$$

If $S'=\{x_0, x_2\}$ and $T'=\{x_1\}$,

$$C_u(C_u(\{x_0, x_2\}) \cup C_u(\{x_1\})) = C_u(\{x_2\} \cup \{x_1\}) = C_u(\{x_1, x_2\}) = \{x_1\}.$$

This illustrates the source of the waste of resources in agenda manipulation that we encountered in Example 8.

The same thing crops up here in Example 10. Consider the choice function that we calculated right after Exercise 137 to illustrate the workings of Example 10. If $S=\{x, y, w\}$ and $T=\{z\}$, then

$$C_u(C_u(\{x, y, w\}) \cup C_u(\{z\})) = C_u(\{x, y, w\} \cup \{z\}) = C_u(\{x, y, w, z\}) = \{z\}.$$

On the other hand if $S'=\{y, z\}$ and $T'=\{x, w\}$, then

$$C_u(C_u(\{y, z\}) \cup C_u(\{x, w\})) = C_u(\{y\} \cup \{w\}) = C_u(\{y, w\}) = \{y\}.$$

The ultimate choice from v depends upon what "path" of decisions on subagendas of v is taken. If this doesn't happen, if you get the same choice no matter how v is broken up, then we say the rule satisfies *independence of path*. Formally, we require that for all u and all v, then for every pair of nonempty S, T with $v=S \cup T$

$$C_u(C_u(S) \cup C_u(T)) = C_u(v).$$

Both Examples 8 and 10 violate independence of path.

Notice that we would have satisfaction of independence of path for decisions made by individuals who are assumed to choose on the basis of their preference orderings in the following way:

$$C^i(v) = \{x \in v \; / \; xR_iy \text{ for all } y \in v\}).$$

Suppose $v=S \cup T$; we want to show that

$$C^i(v) \subset C^i(C^i(S) \cup C^i(T)) \text{ and}$$
$$C^i(C^i(S) \cup C^i(T)) \subset C^i(v).$$

For the first, let $x \in C^i(v)$. Then xR_iy for all $y \in v$. In particular, xR_iy for all $y \in S$ and all $y \in T$. Hence $x \in C^i(S) \cup C^i(T)$. But $C^i(S) \cup C^i(T) \subset S \cup T=v$ and so xR_iy for all $y \in C^i(S) \cup C^i(T)$. Therefore

$$x \in C^i(C^i(S) \cup C^i(T)).$$

To obtain the opposite inclusion, suppose

$$x \in C^i(C^i(S) \cup C^i(T)).$$

To show $x \in C^i(v)$, since clearly $x \in v$, we need only show xR_iy for all $y \in v$. So let $y \in v$. Then $y \in S$ or $y \in T$. Without loss of generality, suppose $y \in S$. Let $z \in C^i(S)$. Then since $z \in C_i(S) \cup C^i(T)$ and $x \in C^i(C^i(S) \cup C^i(T))$ we have xR_iz. Since $z \in C^i(S)$ and $y \in S$ we have zR_iy. Using transitivity of R_i we get xR_iy. Thus we can guarantee satisfaction of independence of path if each choice function can be "explained" as making choices based on a transitive preference relation.

Another way of seeing the problem with Example 10 (and of Example 6) comes by examining a condition weaker than independence of path, namely the consistency condition raised back in Chapter 5. A choice function C is said to satisfy the consistency property called *Property* α (Property 'alpha') if for every agenda $v' \subset v$ whenever an alternative $x \in v'$ is chosen from the larger set, $x \in C(v)$, then it is chosen from the smaller agenda v': $x \in C(v')$. "If the champion of the world is a Pakistani, he must be the champion of Pakistan."

Some of the choice functions generated by Examples 6 and 10 fail to satisfy Property α. With Example 6 we had

$$C_u(\{x_0, x_1, x_2\}) = \{x_2\} \text{ but } x_2 \notin C_u(\{x_1, x_2\}) = \{x_1\}.$$

With Example 10 we had

$$C_u(\{x, y, z, w\}) = \{z\} \text{ but } z \notin C_u(\{y, z\}) = \{y\}.$$

Exercises.
142. Show that if a rule satisfies independence of path then it must satisfy Property α
143. Show that the following choice function satisfies Property α but *not* independence of path:

$$C(\{a, b, c\}) = \{a\},$$
$$C(\{a, b\}) = \{a\}, C(\{a, c\}) = \{a, c\}, C(\{b, c\}) = \{c\}.$$

As we saw in our discussion of choices made by individuals, if choices can be "explained" by a transitive, complete and reflexive preference ordering then the rule satisfies independence of path. Exercise 142 now shows us that such a rule also satisfies this consistency Property α. Considerations like these lead us to the following. A choice function C is *explicable* or *explainable* if there exists a relation Ω such that

$$C(v) = \{x \in v \ / \ x\Omega y \text{ for all } y \in v\}.[4]$$

If the part of the standard domain constraint that requires admissibility of all finite agendas is not satisfied, then there may be a lot of flexibility in explaining C by different relations. For example, if $X = \{x, y, z\}$ and the only admissible agendas are $\{x, y\}$ and $\{x, y, z\}$ with $C(\{x, y\}) = \{y\}$ and $C(\{x, y, z\}) = \{z\}$, then the choice function is explicable by the relation

$$y\Omega x, \ y\Omega y, \ z\Omega x, \ z\Omega y \text{ and } z\Omega z$$

(which *fails all* of reflexivity, completeness and transitivity) or by the relation

$$y\Omega x, \ y\Omega y, \ x\Omega x, \ z\Omega x, \ z\Omega y, \text{ and } z\Omega z$$

(which *satisfies all* of reflexivity, completeness and transitivity). As shorthand, we will say C has a *transitive explanation* if there is a reflexive, complete and transitive Ω such that

---

[4] This Ω is a construct for explaining a choice function; it should *not* be interpreted as a "social preference ordering." As observed in footnote 1, preference is assumed in this text to connect with an individual, not a group.

$$C(v) = \{x \in v \mid x\Omega y \text{ for all } y \in v\}.$$

In turn, we say a social choice rule has *transitive explanations* if at every admissible profile u the associated C_u has a transitive explanation.

Exercises.

144. Show there exists a choice function which is defined on all agendas and which satisfies independence of path but which does not have a transitive explanation.

145. Let the domain of C be all nonempty subsets of $\{a, b, c\}$ with

$$C(\{a, b\}) = \{a, b\}, \; C(\{b, c\}) = \{b, c\}, \; C(\{a, c\}) = \{a\}$$
$$C(\{a, b, c\}) = \{a, b\}.$$

Show C has a reflexive and complete explanation but does *not* have a transitive explanation.

146. Prove: If C has an explanation (not necessarily transitive) and if both v and C(v) are in the domain of C then

$$C(C(v)) = C(v).$$

In each of Exercises 147–151 show that the stated relation is a transitive explanation for C_u in the rule of the indicated example.

147. Example 1: $x\Omega y$ for all x and y.

148. Example 2: $x_i \Omega x_j$ if and only if $i \leq j$.

149. Example 4: $x\Omega y$ if and only if y is not Pareto superior to x.

150. Example 6: $x\Omega y$ if and only if there are alternatives $y_1, y_2, \ldots, y_t$ in X such that

$$N(xR_iy_1) \geq N(y_1R_ix), \; N(y_1R_iy_2) \geq N(y_2R_iy_1), \; \ldots, \; N(y_tR_iy) \geq N(yR_iy_t).$$

151. Example 9: $x\Omega y$ if and only if $r(x) \leq r(y)$ where $r(x)$ is the Borda count of x.

152. Show that *none* of Examples 3, 5, 7, 8 or 10 has a transitive explanation.

153. Suppose a social choice rule $f: u \to C_u$ is such that C_u has all pairs of alternatives in its domain. Construct from C_u the relation Ω^u as follows:

$$x\Omega^u y \text{ if and only if } x \in C_u(\{x, y\}).$$

Show that if C_u has an explanation, Ω^u is one.

154. Suppose a social choice rule $f: u \to C_u$ satisfies the standard domain constraint. Construct from C_u the relation Φ^u as follows:

Define $X_1 = C_u(X)$
$X_2 = C_u(X-X_1)$
$X_3 = C_u(X - (X_1 \cup X_2))$
$\vdots$

$x\Phi^u y$ if and only if $i \leq j$ where $x \in X_i$ and $y \in X_j$.

Show that if C_u has an explanation, Φ^u is one.

155. Suppose that a social choice rule $f: u \to C_u$ satisfies the standard domain constraint. Then if it has an explanation, it has only one; in particular, $\Omega^u = \Phi^u$ then.

Be careful that you see clearly the difference between transitive explanation and independence of irrelevant alternatives. One way to help you remember is to know that in checking independence you fix the agenda and vary the profile while in checking transitive explanation you fix the profile and vary the agenda.

We are now in position to present, in the next Chapter, what was historically the first of the impossibility results in social choice theory, a theorem by Kenneth Arrow.

Further Reading

An excellent readable supplement to this material is Chapters 1 and 1* to 5 and 5* in Amartya K. Sen's *Collective Choice and Social Welfare* (Holden-Day, 1970). Later chapters of Sen's book are also relevant to later material in this text.

Chapter 7. Arrow's Impossibility Theorem

> Arthur C. Clarke's Second Law:
> The only way to find the limits
> of the possible is to go beyond
> them into the impossible.

Let's right away jump in and see the theorem that is the focus of this chapter.

Theorem (Arrow[1]) There *does not exist any* social choice rule satisfying all of:

1. the standard domain constraint;
2. the strong Pareto condition;
3. independence of irrelevant alternatives;
4. has transitive explanations;
5. absence of a dictator.

It is not just that it is *difficult* to find a social choice rule that satisfies all these. We already know it is difficult; we have looked at more than a dozen rules many of which seemed at first to embody important aspects of our ideas of democracy and collective choice but none have satisfied all five properties. No, it isn't just that it is hard; it is *impossible.*

This is really an astonishing result. The conditions do not, on first consideration, seem at odds with one another. And we know from the first section of the previous chapter that we have "countless" billions on billions of conceivable social choice rules to work with.

What's worse, this is a very short list of criteria for a social choice rule. We might want much more than this. We might want each $C_u(v)$ to be a singleton; we wish to provide incentives for individuals to tell the truth about preferences. We might, for that matter, wish to introduce very special assignments of power to individuals or groups of individuals – to endow some people with decisiveness between some alternatives. For example, we might want to endow some individuals the right to *decline* being chosen to elective office even if we don't endow them with the right to be the one chosen. But if we can't find a social choice rule satisfying all of Arrow's criteria, then we certainly can't find a social choice rule satisfying those *plus some more!*

What is especially disturbing about Arrow's theorem is that each of the properties seems on the surface to be desirable, as we have discussed in Chapter 6. But if you still are bothered by some, like having transitive explanations or indepen-

---

[1] The theorem first appeared in "A Difficulty in the Concept of Social Welfare, " *Journal of Political Economy,* Vol. 58, No. 4 (August, 1950) and then in the first edition of Arrow's *Social Choice and Individual Values* (Wiley, 1951). Those versions, however, were shown to be incorrect by Julian Blau; a corrected version appeared in the second edition of Arrow's book (Wiley, 1968).

dence of irrelevant alternatives, be on warning that there are other impossibility results that don't use them. In Chapter 10 we will present an impossibility result concerning the criterion of no one having an incentive to submit false preferences; in Chapter 8 we will present an impossibility result about endowing some people with narrowly constrained power. Neither of these later impossibility results will use either transitive explanations or independence of irrelevant alternatives.

In order to separate out some of the messy details from a proof of Arrow's theorem, we will first establish preliminary results called contagion theorems. To express these contagion results we need one further definition. A set $S \subset N$ is *locally decisive* for alternative x against alternative y if, whenever profile u satisfies

$$\text{i) } xR_iy \text{ for all } i \in S;$$
$$\text{ii) } xP_iy \text{ for at least one } i \in S;$$
$$\text{iii) } yP_jx \text{ for all } j \in N\text{-}S,$$

then $x \in v$ implies $y \notin C_u(v)$. So a locally decisive set has exclusionary power but not as much power as a decisive set. If S is locally decisive for x against y, S can exclude y (if x is available and members of S prefer x to y) but this exclusion is only known to take effect when everyone else, everyone outside S, is strongly opposed, strictly preferring y to x. A set that is *decisive* for x against y has exclusionary power no matter what pattern of preferences on x and y are held by individuals outside S. Sometimes to emphasize this we will say a decisive set is *globally* decisive. That is not a new concept just a stress on a special aspect of our old decisiveness concept. We build this distinction between local and global decisiveness into our notation. If a set S is *locally* decisive for x against y we will write xD_Sy; if S is *globally* decisive for x against y we write xD^*_Sy.

Exercises.

156. If S is (globally) decisive for x against y, then S is locally decisive for x against y.

157. Construct a social choice rule such that there is an S, an x and a y such that S is locally decisive for x against y but not (globally) decisive for x against y.

First Narrow Contagion Result. Suppose with at least three individuals and at least three alternatives a social choice rule satisfies all of

1) the standard domain constraint;
2) the strong Pareto condition;
3) independence of irrelevant alternatives and
4) has transitive explanations.

If for this rule a set S is locally decisive for a against b, then S is globally decisive for a against c where a, b and c are distinct alternatives in X.

Proof. We assume aD_Sb and wish to prove aD^*_Sc. To prove aD^*_Sc, we must show $a \in v$ implies $c \notin C_u(v)$ at *any* profile u where everyone in S finds a to be at least as good as c and one strictly prefers a. So let u be such a profile and partition

S into S_1 and S_2, $S = S_1 \cup S_2$, where everyone in S_1 has $aP_i c$ and everyone (if there *is* anyone) in S_2 has $aI_i c$. So profile u restricted to {a, c} is

$$S_1: ac$$
$$S_2: (ac)$$
$$N\text{-}S: [ac]$$

where the notation [ac] means the members of N-S may have any orderings of a and c (different members of N-S may have different orderings of these two alternatives). We wish to show that a $\in$ v implies $\notin$ c $C_u(v)$. Since C_u has some transitive explanation by Ω, it is equivalent to show $a\Omega c$ and not $c\Omega a$. By Exercise 155, since the standard domain constraint is satisfied, there is a *unique* Ω that can explain C_u, namely

$$x\Omega y \text{ if and only if } x \in C_u(\{x, y\}).$$

So it is sufficient here to prove $C_u(\{a, c\}) = \{a\}$. To prove *this*, we turn our attention to a new profile, constructed so as to be very closely related to u. Profile u', restricted to {a, b, c}, is

$$S_1: abc$$
$$S_2: (abc)$$
$$N\text{-}S: b[ac].$$

(The notation b[ac] is intended to convey the idea that for any j $\in$ N-S, whatever j's preferences may be between a and c *at u*, they are the same here *at u'*.) By the standard domain constraint, the social choice rule yields a choice function $C_{u'}$ at profile u'. Another application of the domain constraint tells us {a, b}, {a, c} and {b, c} are in the domain of $C_{u'}$. By the local decisiveness of S for a against b (and seeing at u' that everybody in S finds a at least as good as b, someone in S_1 strictly prefers a to b and everyone outside S strictly prefers b to a) we get $C_{u'}(\{a, b\}) = \{a\}$. From the strong Pareto condition (and seeing at u' that everyone finds b to be at least as good as c and that someone in S_1 strictly prefers b to c) we get $C_{u'}(\{b, c\}) = \{b\}$.

From $C_{u'}(\{a, b\}) = \{a\}$ and $C_{u'}(\{b, c\}) = \{b\}$ we wish to derive $C_{u'}(\{a, c\}) = \{a\}$. To do this, we must exploit our knowing that $C_{u'}$ has some reflexive, complete and transitive explanation, Ω'. From $C_{u'}(\{a, b\}) = \{a\}$ we get $a\Omega'b$; from $C_{u'}(\{b, c\}) = \{b\}$ we get $b\Omega'c$. These, with transitivity of Ω', imply $a\Omega'c$. By reflexivity, $a\Omega'a$. Together with the fact that Ω' explains $C_{u'}$, these tell us a $\in$ $C_{u'}(\{a, c\})$. To complete our proof that $C_{u'}(\{a, c\}) = \{a\}$, we must show c $\notin$ $C_{u'}(\{a, c\})$. But if it were, then $c\Omega'a$. Since also $b\Omega'c$, we would have by transitivity that $b\Omega'a$. Together with $b\Omega'b$, this would tell us b $\in$ $C_{u'}(\{a, b\})$ which isn't true. Therefore, c $\notin$ $C_{u'}(\{a, c\})$ and so $C_{u'}(\{a, c\}) = \{a\}$. Finally, since u and u' agree on {a, c}, one application of independence of irrelevant alternatives yields

$$C_u(\{a, c\}) = \{a\},$$

which was our goal. ∎

Already it must be apparent that something strange can be obtained from four of Arrow's conditions. We may very well wish to endow some group with power between a and b without endowing them with power between a and some third possibly unrelated alternative.

Second Narrow Contagion Result. Suppose with at least three individuals and at least three alternatives a social choice rule satisfies all of

1) the standard domain constraint;
2) the strong Pareto condition;
3) independence of irrelevant alternatives and
4) has transitive explanations.

If for this rule a set S is locally decisive for a against b, then S is globally decisive for c against b where a, b and c are distinct alternatives in X.

Exercise.
158. Prove this second contagion result. [Your proof can be closely patterned after the proof of the first contagion result.]

Broad Contagion Result. Suppose with at least three individuals and at least three alternatives a social choice rule satisfies all of

1) the standard domain constraint;
2) the strong Pareto condition;
3) independence of irrelevant alternatives and
4) has transitive explanations.

If for this rule a set S is locally decisive for one alternative against another, then S is globally decisive between any two alternatives.

Proof. Let us suppose that xD_Sy; we wish to prove zD^*_Sw where z and w are any two alternatives in X. Our proof will work in two parts, first showing broad contagion over a *triple* of alternatives and then using this to show broad contagion over all of X.

Part 1. We have xD_Sy. Let t be any third alternative in X. We wish to show that D^*_S holds between any two alternatives in $\{x, y, t\}$. We already have part of this. The first narrow contagion result plus xD_Sy gives

$$xD^*_St; \tag{1}$$

the second narrow contagion result gives

$$tD^*_Sy. \tag{2}$$

But from Exercise 156, xD^*_St implies xD_St. This combines with the first narrow contagion result to give

$$xD^*_Sy; \tag{3}$$

and combines with the second narrow contagion result to give

$$yD^*_St. \tag{4}$$

From this last and another application of Exercise 156 we get yD_St. By the first narrow contagion result,

$$yD^*_Sx. \tag{5}$$

Finally, from (2), tD^*_Sy, an application of Exercise 156 gives tD_Sy and a last application of the first narrow contagion result gives

$$tD^*_Sx. \tag{6}$$

Together, (1) to (6) ensure that xD_Sy implies D^*_S holds between any pair from $\{x, y, t\}$.

Part 2. We continue to assume xD_Sy. Let w and z be any two alternatives. If one or both of them is in $\{x, y\}$ then in Part 1 we showed zD^*_Sw. So we need only consider the case where $\{z, w\}$ doesn't overlap at all with $\{x, y\}$. Look first at $\{x, y, z\}$. Part 1 tells us that we can conclude xD^*_Sz. From xD^*_Sz, Exercise 156 gives xD_Sz. Using this and looking at $\{x, w, z\}$, we apply Part 1 to get zD^*_Sw. ∎

Clearly, something has gone wildly wrong if limited (local) power over one pair of alternatives spreads to all pairs of alternatives and there with enhanced (global) power. The Arrow theorem is really just a way of dramatically expressing a consequence of contagion.

Proof of Arrow's Theorem. We are going to assume there does exist a social choice rule satisfying all of Arrow's conditions and use this assumption to discover a contradiction. That will mean our assumption is false.

By the strong Pareto condition, there exist decisive sets. Let S be a decisive set of smallest size (if there is more than one, just pick one arbitrarily). By the no dictator condition, S has at least two members. Reach into S and pick out one individual we will call i. Then S-{i} is still nonempty. Consider a profile u restricted to three alternatives in X as follows

$$\begin{array}{l} i: xyz \\ S-\{i\}: yzx \\ N\text{-}S: zxy. \end{array}$$

(Recall the voting paradox profile.)

The contradiction we seek (from assuming Arrow's conditions) will take form here by showing that i must be a dictator. By the broad contagion result, it is sufficient to show that i is locally decisive for x against z. By independence of irrelevant alternatives, it would suffice to show that at u, $C_u(\{x, z\}) = \{x\}$ for then x alone would be chosen from $\{x, z\}$ at any profile that, like u, has i strictly preferring x to z and every one else strictly opposed.

Since S is decisive, $C_u(\{y, z\}) = \{y\}$. If $C_u(\{x, y\}) = \{y\}$, then independence of irrelevant alternatives would tell us S-{i} is locally decisive for y against x. But then the broad contagion result would tell us that S-{i} is decisive, contrary to our choice of S as a minimal decisive set. Hence $C_u(\{x, y\}) \neq \{y\}$, i.e., $x \in C_u(\{x, y\})$. Remember C_u is explainable by a complete, reflexive transitive Ω. From $x \in C_u(\{x, y\})$ we see $x\Omega y$. From $C_u(\{y, z\}) = \{y\}$, we see $y\Omega z$. Transitivity yields $x\Omega z$; hence $x \in C_u(\{x, z\})$. It only remains to show $z \notin C_u(\{x, z\})$. But if so, then $z\Omega x$ which with $x\Omega y$ would tell us $z\Omega y$ which we know is false from $C_u(\{y, z\}) = \{y\}$. Hence $C_u(\{x, z\}) = \{x\}$ which we have noted, implies i is a dictator. We were led to this contradiction by the assumption that there is a social choice rule satisfying all of Arrow's conditions. So that assumption is false. There is no social choice rule satisfying all. ∎

Exercises.

159. For each of the social choice rule Examples 1 to 10 in Chapter 6, list which of the conditions in Arrow's theorem is violated by that rule.

160. Here is a social choice rule designed by the British mathematician Charles Dodgson (better known as Lewis Carroll of *Alice in Wonderland* fame):

For each profile u, calculate for each alternative x a score, $s_u(x)$ as follows: for each alternative y in X such that y defeats x by simple majority vote, look at the excess amount by which y wins,

$$N(yP_ix) - N(xP_iy).$$

Add these excesses up to get the score,

$$s_u(x) = \sum[N(yP_ix) - N(xP_iy)] \text{ over all } y$$
$$\text{such that } N(yP_ix) > N(xP_iy).$$

Then, from agenda v, choose those alternatives with minimum score:

$$C_u(v) = \{x \in v \ / \ s_u(x) \le s_u(y) \text{ for all } y \in v\}.$$

a. Determine what this rule has selected from $v = \{x, y, z\}$ at the voter paradox profile:

$$1: xyz$$
$$2: yzx$$
$$3: zxy.$$

b. Which of Arrow's conditions is violated by Dodgson's rule?

Since Arrow's theorem tells us each social choice rule has some problems, it is natural to try to take several and "patch" them together to try avoiding problems each has separately. For example, we have seen that the Condorcet winner rule seems appealing where it works, but that it sometimes fails to choose anything (i.e., it fails to satisfy the standard domain constraint). We can think of repairing this by patching it up when necessary with a Borda rule (which *does* satisfy the standard domain constraint). For example, consider the following rule which we shall call the *Local Borda Patch:*

$$C_u(v) = \begin{cases} \text{the set of Condorcet winners, if there are any.} \\ \\ \text{the set determined by the local Borda rule if no} \\ \text{Condorcet winner exists at v.} \end{cases}$$

It must be understood that this kind of patching is *not* a route around Arrow's theorem. A patched-up rule is still a rule and must violate at least one of Arrow's conditions.

Exercises.

161. Which of Arrow's conditions are violated by the Local Borda Patch?
162. Here is a *Global Borda Patch:*

$$C_u(v) = \begin{cases} \text{the set of Condorcet winners if there } \textit{are} \text{ Condorcet winners for} \\ \quad \text{every v at this u} \\ \text{the set determined by the global Borda rule if, for even one v,} \\ \quad \text{there is no Condorcet winner at u.} \end{cases}$$

Which of Arrow's conditions are violated by the Global Borda Patch?

163. Which of Arrow's conditions are violated by the Kramer Rule? (See Exercise 84).
164. Given a set S and ordering R, let the *bottom* B(S, R) be the set of elements of S at the bottom of R restricted to S:

$$B(S, R) = \{x \in S \ / \ y \in S \text{ implies } yRx\}.$$

Given a set S and profile $u = (R_1, \ldots, R_n)$, the *plurality worst* elements PW(S, u) are those at the bottom of at least as many orderings as any others:

$$PW(S, u) =$$
$$\{x \in S \ / \ |\{i/x \in B(S, R_i)\}| \geq |\{i/y \in B(S, R_i)\}| \text{ for all } y \in S\}.$$

Then a rule of *rejecting-the-worst* is constructed as follows given a profile u and non-empty set v of alternatives:
Calculate PW(v, u). If this is not all of v, set

$$v_1 = v \ - \ PW(v, u).$$

Calculate $PW(v_1, u)$. If this is not all of v_1, set

$$v_2 = v_1 \ - \ PW(v_1, u).$$

Continue in this fashion until you reach the first k with

$$PW(v_k, u) = v_k.$$

Then $C_u(v) = v_k$.

Which of Arrow's conditions are violated by the rule of rejecting-the-worst?

165. Let a and b be two of the many alternatives in X. Consider the social choice rule[2] f that assigns at profile u the choice function

$$C_u(v) = \{x \in v \ / \ xR^u y \text{ for all } y \in v\}$$

where R^u is defined as follows:

$$xR_u y \text{ just when } \begin{cases} \{x, y\} \neq \{a, b\} \text{ and } xR_3y; \\ \{x, y\} = \{a, b\} \text{ and } xR_iy \text{ for all } i. \end{cases}$$

Thus individual #3 determines R^u except on $\{a, b\}$ where unanimity determine R^u. Show that this rule satisfies all of Arrow's conditions except that the explanation R^u is not transitive. Show, however, that R^u *does* satisfy *acyclicity:*

$$x_1 P^u x_2 \text{ and } x_2 P^u x_3 \text{ and } \ldots \text{ and } x_{n-1} P^u x_n \text{ imply } x_1 R^u x_n.$$

Further Reading

The literature on Arrow's theorem is large. Before tackling Arrow's own *Social Choice and Individual Values*, you might try the easier *Arrow's Theorem: The Paradox of Social Choice* (Yale, 1980) by Alfred MacKay who has an engaging analogy between aggregating preferences into a social choice rule and aggregating performances in decathlon events into an overall score. (Be careful, though, as MacKay follows an early confusion of Arrow's between independence of irrelevant alternatives and explicability.) My own favorite, of course, is Jerry Kelly's *Arrow Impossibility Theorems* (Academic, 1978).

---

[2] This example is from Douglas H. Blair and Robert Pollak, "Acyclic Collective Choice Rules," *Econometrica, Vol.* 50, No. 4 (July, 1982) p. 932.

Chapter 8. Power

Now we aim at a quite different set of results that depend entirely on power properties of social choice rules. Because stipulations of who has what power seem more central to our political philosophy concerns than transitive explanations or independence of irrelevant alternatives, the impossibility results of this chapter may strike you as more dramatic than Arrow's theorem.

The concept of power we work with here is the decisiveness power to exclude alternatives from chosen sets. It is a property of many social choice procedures that exclusionary power is assigned to just single individuals or to coalitions of less than all individuals. For example, in filling public offices we normally grant potential candidates the power to decline nomination. (And if we worry about all possible profiles of preferences, what do we do if everyone declines nomination?)

A coalition $S \subset N$ is decisive *between* alternatives x and y if S is decisive for x against y and also for y against x. A social choice rule satisfies *Sen's weak power condition*[1] if and only if there is an individual, i, and a pair of alternatives, x, y, such that {i} is decisive between x and y and there is another, different individual, j, and a pair of alternatives, w, z, such that {j} is decisive between w and z. The adjective "weak" in this terminology is to alert us that we would usually want a more comprehensive assignment of power. Here we are allocating power to just two individuals and, for each, between just one pair of alternatives. We might normally want to extend exclusionary power to more individuals or coalitions and, for each, to more than just one pair of alternatives; but for what we plan to do next we needn't impose such stringent requirements on a rule. If it proves difficult (impossible) to carry out even this much power allocation, how much harder it would be to assign still more decisiveness to coalitions. Also note that while in the definition of Sen's weak power condition we require that individuals i and j be distinct we aren't insisting that z and w be distinct from x and y.

Exercises.

166. Look back at the social choice rules of Examples 1 to 10 in Chapter 6 and find a case where there is an individual i and a pair of alternatives, x, y, such that {i} is decisive for x against y but *not* for y against x.
167. Which of Examples 1 to 10 in Chapter 6 satisfy Sen's weak power condition?

---

[1] Sen originally called this "weak minimal liberalism."

168. Consider the following social choice rule where $X = \{w, x, y, z\}$. At profile $u = (R_1, R_2, \ldots, R_n)$, the rule yields C_u where $C_u(v) = v'$ where v' is the *largest* subset of v consistent with the following rules:

> i) if $x \in v$ and xP_1y, then $y \notin v'$;
> ii) if $y \in v$ and yP_1x, then $x \notin v'$;
> iii) if $w \in v$ and wP_2z, then $z \notin v'$;
> iv) if $z \in v$ and zP_2w, then $w \notin v'$.

Show that this social choice rule satisfies Sen's weak power condition *and* the standard domain constraint.

169. Show that this rule violates the Pareto condition.

This last exercise is our entree to a theorem due to the economist and philosopher Amartya Sen of Harvard University. Sen called this the Impossibility of a Paretian Liberal.

Theorem (Sen[2]). There does not exist a social choice rule satisfying all of

1) the standard domain constraint;
2) the weak Pareto condition;
3) Sen's weak power condition.

Proof. As remarked above, we have not assumed $\{x, y\}$ and $\{w, z\}$ are disjoint; this forces us to design a proof around several cases.

Case 1. $\{x, y\}$ and $\{w, z\}$ have *two* elements in common, say $x = z$ and $y = w$. Then the power condition amounts to the requirement that *both* i and j are decisive between x and y. Consider the following profile u (restricted to x and y):

$$i: xy;$$
$$j: yx;$$
$$\text{others}: xy.$$

Then $C_u(\{x, y\})$ can't contain x since j is decisive for y against x and it can't contain y since i is decisive for x against y. But $C_u(\{x, y\}) = \emptyset$ shows a violation of the standard domain constraint. (No use is made of the Pareto condition for this first Case.)

Case 2. $\{x, y\}$ and $\{w, z\}$ have exactly *one* element in common, say $x = z$. Here the power condition amounts to the requirement that i is decisive between x and y while j is decisive between x and w. Consider the following profile u (restricted to $\{x, y, w\}$):

$$i: xyw;$$
$$rj: ywx;$$
$$\text{others}: xyw.$$

Then $x \notin C_u(\{x, y, w\})$ since j excludes x in favor of w; $y \notin C_u(\{x, y, w\})$ since i excludes y in favor of x; $w \notin C_u(\{x, y, w\})$ since y is available and is Pareto superior to w.

---

[2] Sen, Amartya K., "The Impossibility of a Paretian Liberal," *Journal of Political Economy* Vol. 78, No. 1 (January/February, 1970), pp. 152-157.

Case 3. {x, y} and {z, w} have *no* elements in common.
Consider the following restricted profile u:

$$i: wxyz;$$
$$j: yzwx;$$
$$\text{others: } wxyz.$$

Then $C_u(\{x, y, z, w\})$ can't contain y because of i's exclusion of y in favor of x; j excludes w in favor of z; x loses to Pareto superior w and z loses to Pareto superior y. So $C_u(\{x, y, z, w\}) = \emptyset$ and the standard domain constraint is violated. ■

Exercises.
170. Show that if in the definition of Sen's weak power condition we replace {i} and {j} by any two *disjoint non-empty* subsets S_1 and S_2 of N we get an analogous theorem.
171. If we are willing to impose the condition that {w, z} and {x, y} are disjoint, we no longer have to require that i and j are decisive *between* the elements of their pair. Define the *modified weak power condition* as follows:
There is an individual i, and a pair of alternatives x, y, such that i is decisive for x against y and another individual j, j ≠ i, and a pair of alternatives z, w, disjoint from {x,y}, such that j is decisive for w against z.
Prove there does not exist a social choice rule satisfying all of:

1) the standard domain constraint;
2) the weak Pareto condition;
3) the modified power condition with $X = \{x, y, z, w\}$.

Two stories are often told around the presentation of Sen's theorem and these two interpretations will be taken up in the next chapter when we examine responses to the impossibility of a Paretian liberal. The first story is due to Sen and the second to Allan Gibbard.

Story # 1. There is just a single copy of *Lady Chatterly's Lover* and only time enough left for at most one person to read it. There are two individuals, Mr. A (the prude) and Mr. B (the lascivious). The three alternatives, then, are:

r_A, A alone reads the book;
r_B, B alone reads the book;
r_0, no one reads the book.

We assume a social choice rule in which each individual has the power to *not* read the book and each individual has the power to read it if the other doesn't read it; i.e., A is decisive between r_A and r_0 and B is decisive between r_B and r_0. Also, the set of both individuals is decisive between any pair of alternatives (the Pareto condition is satisfied). We explore what happens at the profile

A: $r_0 r_A r_B$;
B: $r_A r_B r_0$.

The prude wishes most that no one read Lawrence, but if someone is to read it, he would rather it were himself, keeping B from being exposed to its pornography. Lascivious B wants *someone* to read the book; preferably Mr. A (perhaps to educate him away from his reactionary preferences, perhaps just to embarrass him). With agenda $\{r_0, r_A, r_B\}$, we see that r_0 won't be chosen since B prefers r_B and is decisive between r_B and r_0. Also, r_A won't be chosen since A prefers r_0 and is decisive between r_A and r_0. Finally, r_B won't be chosen since r_A is Pareto superior. The choice set is empty.

Story # 2. There are three individuals, Edwin, Angelina and the judge. The three alternatives are:

w_E, Angelina marries Edwin and the judge remains single;

w_J, Angelina marries the judge and Edwin remains single;

w_0, all three remain single.

Now we suppose a social choice rule that satisfies the Pareto condition and which operates after the judge offers to marry Angelina and so cedes to her the power of decisiveness between w_J and w_0. Edwin has the power to decline marriage – he is decisive for w_0 against w_E. Consider the profile:

$$A: w_E w_J w_0;$$
$$E: w_0 w_E w_J;$$
$$J: w_E w_J w_0.$$

Angelina wants to marry, preferably Edwin. The judge wants whatever Angelina wants. Edwin wants to remain single, but would marry Angelina to keep her from the judge. w_0 isn't chosen, for Angelina would exclude that in favor of marrying the judge; w_J isn't chosen as w_E is Pareto superior; w_E isn't chosen as Edwin would exclude that in favor of w_0. The choice set is empty.

Before we turn in the next chapter to responses to Sen's result, we present a theorem closely related to his but which depends for its expression on understanding the "internal structure" of alternatives. With one exception, "alternative" has been treated in this text as a primitive, unanalyzed concept. (The one exception was in discussing the pure distribution problem where alternatives were lists of allocations of some commodity.) Now we will assume that an alternative is a *list* of outcomes on t different issues indicated by a square bracket notation:

$$x = [x_1, x_2, ..., x_t].$$

Corresponding to each issue k, $1 \leq k \leq t$, there is a set M_k of possible outcomes and the set X is all possible lists made out of these outcomes:

$$X = \{[x_1, ..., x_t] \, / \, x_1 \in M_1, ..., x_t \in M_t\}.$$

We assume each M_k contains at least two elements.

As with profiles, we say two alternatives $x = [x_1, ..., x_t]$ and $y = [y_1, ..., y_t]$ are *k-variants* if x and y differ on, at most, the *kth* issue:

$$\text{for all } j \neq k \text{ we have } x_j = y_j.$$

A social choice rule will be said to satisfy *Property L* if and only if for each individual b there is at least one issue k such that b is decisive between any two k-variants.

Exercise.

172. Show that if a rule satisfies Property L then it satisfies Sen's weak power condition.

Since, by Exercise 172, Property L is stronger than Sen's weak power condition, we might, after substitution of Property L for the power condition in Sen's theorem, expect to be able to relax some of the other conditions. We can. Let's throw away the Pareto condition entirely.

Theorem (Gibbard[3]). There does not exist a social choice rule satisfying both the standard domain constraint and Property L.

Proof. Without loss of generality, let's suppose that individual #1 is decisive between any two 1-variants and #2 is decisive between any two 2-variants. Choose specific values, $x_3^*, ..., x_t^*$, for all issues except the first two. Let P_1 and W_1 be two possible values of the first issue and P_2, W_2 be two possible values of the second issue. Consider the four alternatives:

$$PP = [P_1, P_2, x_3^*, ..., x_t^*],$$
$$PW = [P_1, W_2, x_3^*, ..., x_t^*],$$
$$WP = [W_1, P_2, x_3^*, ..., x_t^*],$$
$$WW = [W_1, W_2, x_3^*, ..., x_t^*];$$

then look at the profile u restricted to these four alternatives:

$$1: WW\ PP\ PW\ WP$$
$$2: WP\ PW\ WW\ PP$$
$$others: WP\ PW\ WW\ PP.$$

With $v = \{WW, PP, WP, PW\}$ we see

WW $\notin C_u(v)$ since #2 prefers WP to WW and is decisive between them;
PP $\notin C_u(v)$ since #2 prefers PW to PP and is decisive between them;
PW $\notin C_u(v)$ since #1 prefers WW to PW and is decisive between them;
WP $\notin C_u(v)$ since #1 prefers PP to WP and is decisive between them.

So $C_u(v) = \emptyset$, violating the standard domain constraint. ∎

There is also a standard illustrative story around this theorem and proof. Each of two individuals can choose the own bedroom wall color, either white (W) or pink (P). Pink on #1's walls and white on #2's would be PW. But they will be unable to select jointly a pair of room colors if #1's preference is that they have identically colored rooms while #2's preference is that they have different colored rooms.

Further Reading

Sen's 1970 article in the *Journal of Political Economy* is both short and rewarding. For a philosophy perspective on these issues and for a "work choice" story to supplement our Lady Chatterly and Angelina stories, see Sen's "Liberty and Social Choice" in the *Journal of Philosophy,* Vol. 80, No. 1 (Jan., 1983) pp. 5–28.

---

[3] Gibbard, Allan, "A Pareto Consistent Libertarian Claim," *Journal of Economic Theory* Vol. 7, No. 4 (April, 1974), pp. 388–410.

Chapter 9. Rights

Of the three conditions in Sen's theorem on the impossibility of a Paretian liberal, two are concerned with power. Both Sen's weak power condition and the Pareto condition endow certain coalitions with some exclusionary decisiveness power. It is not surprising, then, that the main reactions to Sen's theorem have focused on this idea of power.

Describing these reactions will prove easier if we take our power concept and "unpack" it, to show that it really contains three quite different components. To say that a coalition is decisive for x against y as we have defined it is to say three things:

1) S is assigned a *right* to exclude y when x is available.
2) S faces the *constraint* that it is only allowed to exercise this right when everyone in S finds x to be at least as good as y and at least one member of S strictly prefers x to y.
3) S has a decision rule about when it chooses to exercise the rights it has been assigned. In the version we have so far examined, the *rights exercising rule* is the same as the constraint, i.e., S exercises the right every time it *can*. S exercises its right to x over y whenever everyone in S finds x to be at least as good as y and at least one member of S strictly prefers x to y.

Typically, social choice theorists have left the first part of this power idea alone. To the extent that decisiveness entails allocating rights, most theorists agree that exclusionary rights ought to be assigned both to the large coalition of all individuals (as in the Pareto condition) and to coalitions of just single individuals (as in Sen's weak power condition). Of course, these latter assignments make more sense under some interpretations of "alternative" than under others. If we are looking at ordinary legislative proposals in the U. S. Senate, few of us might want to endow single Senators with exclusionary power. If we are looking at procedures for electing officials, we might want to endow individuals with the right to decline nomination, to exclude themselves from serving, but not the opposite right to exclude their not serving. But if we adopt an interpretation of alternative that is very broad and detailed – complete descriptions of potential consumption, production, exchange and inventory situations for all agents in an economy possibly including a description of all interpersonal relationships and both public and private behavior – then the rights allocation parts of the two power assumptions in Sen's theorem seem reasonable. Sen writes of each individual being decisive between two such descriptions that differ only in that in one he sleeps on his stomach and in the other he sleeps on his back. We suppose there is a *rights system* RS, a collection of triples (x, y, S) so that (x, y, S) $\in$ RS means coalition S has the right to x over y. When S is a singleton, {i}, we write (x, y, i) rather than (x, y, {i}).

The second component of our concept, the idea that a coalition faces constraints on when it *can* exercise its rights has seemed a more fruitful place to work. If, as in the proof of Sen's theorem, we find $C_u(v)$ empty because too many coalitions have exercised their exclusionary rights, this could be avoided if there were enough constraints on carrying out exclusions. Of course we have to be careful in that the idea of rights might be totally destroyed if we put too many constraints on this carrying out. What is the sense of a right to x over y if you are constrained so that you can never exercise this right?

Sen himself reacts to this theorem by saying that it is not enough even if everyone in S prefers x to y for them to be allowed to exercise a right to x over y. We must first gather more information than just preferences; especially must we learn about motives behind preferences. In the *Lady Chatterly's Lover* story, the alternative r_B, that the lascivious Mr. B alone reads the book, was excluded by the Pareto condition because everyone preferred r_A, that prudish Mr. A alone reads the book. But Sen would say that these preferences were badly motivated and ought not to count.

It may be argued that it is not merely important to know who prefers what, but also *why* he has this preference. Mr. A does not wish to read the book himself if the choice is between his reading it or no one reading it, but wants to deny Mr. B the advantage of reading it (an advantage that B values vis-a-vis not reading it). This particular nature of A's preference ordering, it could be argued, distracts from the value of A's preference for his reading the book vis-a-vis B reading the book. Preferences based on excessive nosiness about what is good for others, should be, it could be argued, ignored[1].

But there are two difficulties here. The first is obvious; information on motives would seem especially difficult to collect. Even if we always clearly knew our own motives, which certainly isn't true, what incentive would we have to honestly reveal that information if it were going to be used to constrain our rights exercising? Secondly, not all possible motives behind the preferences in the story might be discarded as excessively nosy. Suppose Mr. A, who has a medical background, knows that one more book reading would render Mr. B permanently blind. Not only that, but A knows Mr. B's heart is so weak it would burst if he were told this terrible news about his eyes. Mr. A prefers r_A to r_B to save Mr. B from blindness and heart failure. Would we wish to throw away Mr. A's desire to protect Mr. B? This is an extreme story, but the central point is there – we can't *always* count on motivation information to destroy preference information.

Julian Blau has a preference-based suggestion about a constraint on rights exercising to get around Sen's theorem. The idea is that sometimes an individual's preferences can be *internally* characterized as "meddlesome"; when an individual i has a right but his preference ordering is meddlesome, he is not allowed to carry out his right. Specifically, we associate with each individual i a set D_i of two alternatives between which i is assigned a right. In an ordering R that is reflexive, complete and transitive, we say xPw is stronger than yPz if

[1] Sen, Amartya K., *Collective Choice and Social Welfare* (Holden-Day, 1970) p. 83

i) xRy, yPz, zRw and

ii) one of those R's in part i) is strict preference, P.

Given a profile $u = (R_1, R_2, \ldots, R_n)$, individual i is *meddlesome* at u if

1) he is not indifferent on D_i;
2) there is an individual j such that
   a) j is not indifferent on D_j;
   b) i's strict preference on D_j is opposite j's;
   c) R_i is stronger on D_j than on D_i.

With this framework, Blau proves that if there are two individuals, there *does* exist a social choice rule satisfying all of

1. The standard domain constraint;
2. The Pareto condition;
3. Each i has the property that if x, y $\in D_i$ and, at u, xP_iy then x $\in$ v implies y $\notin C_u(v)$ *if* at least one individual is not meddlesome at u.

There are two main critiques to Blau's resolution of Sen's dilemma. The first is directly concerned with the principle of what part of a meddlesome individual's preferences to ignore. Here is Sen again:

But is this an acceptable solution? Since libertarian values come into their own in defending personal liberty against meddling, one can argue that the presence of meddling makes libertarian values more (*not* less) important. If everyone meddles in the sense of Blau, surely libertarian values should demand that the meddling part of each person's preferences be ignored but the non-meddling parts dealing with one's own affairs be defended against other people's meddling. Indeed, the ingenious consideration of meddlesomeness, so well discussed by Blau, seems to lead naturally to a critique of the part of the individual preferences incorporated in the Pareto relation rather than of the part incorporated in the personal rights, i.e., precisely the opposite of what Blau proposes.

Consider four alternative social states $\{x_1, y_1, x_2, y_2\}$ with $\{x_1, y_1\}$ being person 1's assigned pair and $\{x_2, y_2\}$ being person 2's pair. Let person 1 prefer x_1 to y_1, and person 2 be meddlesome by ordering the four alternatives in the strict descending order: y_1, x_2, y_2, x_1. No one denies 2's right to rank x_2 and y_2 as he likes. If we are upset about his being meddlesome, surely the object of our wrath should be his preference for y_1 over x_2, or for y_2 over x_1, or both. And these are precisely the pairs over which 2's preferences give muscle to the Pareto relation. The same applies to 1; he can be meddlesome by ordering: y_2, x_1, y_1, x_2. No one denies his right to prefer x_1 to y_1 but since he also prefers y_2 to x_1 and y_1 to x_2, he is meddlesome. Once again the finger points towards precisely the same two pairs on which person 1's preference - like person 2's - gives the Pareto relations their content.

We can divide person 2's rankings in the ordering $y_1x_2y_2x_1$ into three ordered pairs, viz., a 'self-regarding' ordered pair $\{x_2, y_2\}$ and two 'non-self-regarding' ordered pairs $\{y_1, x_2\}$ and $\{y_2, x_1\}$. If person 1 happens to prefer x_1 to y_1 then this overall order of person 2 is meddlesome. Given that, we might decide to follow one of the following three ways of discounting meddlesome 2's preference ordering:
(a) ignore his entire ordering;
(b) ignore his ordering over non-self-regarding pairs;
(c) ignore his ordering of the self-regarding pair.

It would seem rather natural to follow (a) or (b), whereas Blau follows (c), whereby the preference is ignored precisely over the pair on which the person in question can be hardly accused of being meddlesome.[2]

---

[2] Sen, Amartya K., "Liberty, Unanimity and Rights," *Economica* Vol. 43 (1976).

A second critique points to the need in Blau's possibility theorem for two individuals. If there are more than two, Blau's suspension of decisiveness won't work even if we say that decisiveness comes into play only if *no one* is meddlesome. Consider the following profile u with three individuals where $D_i = \{a_i, b_i\}$.

$$1: b_3a_1b_2a_3b_1a_2$$
$$2: b_1a_2b_3a_1b_2a_3$$
$$3: b_2a_3b_1a_2b_3a_1.$$

Exercises.

173. Demonstrate that in u no one is meddlesome.

174. Show that $C_u(\{a_1, a_2, a_3, b_1, b_2, b_3\}) = \emptyset$ if both the Pareto condition and Blau's new modified condition are satisfied.

Allan Gibbard has suggested a constraint based on "conditional" preferences rather than meddlesome ones. Gibbard's framework is the one that he developed for last chapter's theorem on Property L. Alternatives are lists $x = [x_1, x_2, ..., x_d]$ of issue values and each individual has an issue k such that he is endowed with the right to choose between k variants. The example used to illustrate the problem with an unconstrained version of rights allocation involved pink walls and white walls with profile

$$1: WW \ PP \ PW \ WP$$
$$2: WP \ PW \ WW \ PP.$$

Individual #1's most preferred alternative, WW, has white walls for #1's room. But #1's preference for white walls over pink is *conditional* upon #2 having white walls. If #2 has white walls, #1 prefers white himself. He prefers WW to PW. But if #2 has pink walls, #1 prefers pink himself. He prefers PP to WP. #1's preferences on his issue are conditional on #2's choices on #2's issue. Similarly here, #2 prefers pink walls if #1 has white (WP is preferred to WW) but white walls if #1 has pink (PW is preferred to PP). Neither has preferences that aren't conditional on the other's choices.

Where M_k is the set of possible values of the *k*th issue, let r and s be distinct elements of M_k. We will say that at profile u, individual b (who has rights on k-variants) *prefers* r to s *unconditionally* if for every pair x, y of k variants with $x_k = r$ and $y_k = s$, xP_by. A social choice rule satisfies *Property L'* if and only if for each individual b there is a k such that whenever x and y are k variants with $x_k = r$ and $y_k = s$ and when b prefers r to s unconditionally, then

$$x \in v \text{ implies } y \notin C_u(v).$$

Gibbard proves that it *is* possible to have a social choice rule that satisfies both the standard domain constraint and Property L'. But he also shows that the cure is not a very good one. Any such rule must violate the Pareto condition.

Theorem (Gibbard). There does not exist a social choice rule satisfying all of:

      (i) the standard domain constraint;
      (ii) the Pareto condition;
      (iii) Property L'.

Proof. Let PP, PW, WP and WW be just what they were last chapter; let condition L' give #1 (weakened) power over 1-variants and #2 over 2-variants. Consider the following profile u restricted to these four alternatives:

$$1: \text{WW PW WP PP}$$
$$2: \text{PP PW WP WW}$$
$$\text{others: WW PW WP PP.}$$

Let $v = \{WW, WP, PW, PP\}$ and consider $C_u(v)$:

PP $\notin C_u(v)$ since WP $\in v$ and #1 prefers W to P unconditionally; PW $\notin C_u(v)$ since PP $\in v$ and #2 prefers P to W unconditionally; WW $\notin C_u(v)$ since WP $\in v$ and #2 prefers P to W unconditionally; WP $\notin C_u(v)$ since v contains p which is Pareto superior to WP. Thus $C_u(v) = \emptyset$ and the standard domain constraint is violated. ∎

The next approach to resolving the Paretian liberal dilemma, another by Allan Gibbard, depends on that third component of decisiveness where a coalition is seen to *decide* whether or not to exercise a right it is allocated and which it is not constrained from carrying out.

To get the underlying idea, let's go back to the Edwin-Angelina-judge example where Edwin's ordering was:

$$E: w_O w_E w_J.$$

Now Edwin is assigned the right to exclude w_E in favor of w_O and until now we have had an *automatic* rights exercising rule. If i has (x, y, i) in rights system RS and $x P_i y$ at u, then $x \in v$ implies $y \notin C_u(v)$. In this example, $(w_O, w_E, \text{Edwin}) \in$ RS and $w_O P_E w_E$ so $w_E \notin C_u(\{w_O, w_E, w_J\})$. But then Edwin watches Angelina exercise her right to w_J over w_O and so, if both Edwin and Angelina choose to exercise their rights $C_u(\{w_O, w_E, w_J\}) = \{w_J\}$. But w_J is Edwin's *least* preferred alternative. In particular, w_J is worse for Edwin than the w_E he was trying to avoid by exercising (w_O, w_E, Edwin). Gibbard's resolution would call for abandonment of the automaticity of Edwin's rights exercising and allow him to decide to waive the right (w_O, w_E, Edwin) that has been allocated to him. We will follow Gibbard in exploring what kinds of rights exercising decision theory might counter Sen's result.

Our approach is a little indirect in that what we will describe will be a rule about rights *waiving*. Rights will then be exercised if they are not waived. Suppose $(x, y, i) \in$ RS. We will say (x, y, i) is in i's *waiver set* $W_i(u, v)$ at profile u and agenda v if the following holds:

There exists a sequence $y_1, y_2, ..., y_g$ in v such that

(i) $y_g = x$
(ii) $y_1 \neq y$
(iii) $y R_i y_1$
(iv) for all t, $1 \leq t \leq g-1$, either
(a) $y_t P_j y_{t+1}$ for all $j \in N$ or
(b) there is a $j \neq i$ with $(y_t, y_{t+1}, j) \in$ RS and $y_t P_j y_{t+1}$.

Gibbard's use of the right's waiving scheme is in the context used earlier of alternatives that are lists of issue values.

Condition L'': For each individual b there is an issue k such that if x and y are two k-variants then (x, y, b) ∈ RS. If

$$\text{(i) (x, y, b) ∈ RS and}$$
$$\text{(ii) } xP_by \text{ and}$$
$$\text{(iii) (x, y, b) } ∉ W_i(u, v)$$

then

$$x ∈ v \text{ implies } y ∉ C_u(v).$$

Gibbard has shown that there *does* exist a social choice rule satisfying the standard domain constraint, the Pareto condition and Condition L''. *But* condition L'' has a lot of problems because the rights waiving rule embodied in it has lots of problems.

1. It places heavy demands on information holding and processing. To decide, i must know all of u, all of RS and must be able to calculate arbitrarily long g-sequences.
2. The rule is extremely cautious. There may be many g-sequences that start up from x and terminate in alternatives that i vastly prefers to y. But if there is just one ending in a no-better-than-y alternative, (x, y, i) is waived.
3. Why would you waive your right to x over y if you can only be forced to a y_1 that you find indifferent with y? (Gibbard agrees if you are indifferent because $y_1 = y$ but that is very narrow). Why not change (ii) and (iii) in the waiver set definition to yP_iy_1?
4. L'' doesn't allow for repairing sequences. Suppose i is considering exercising (x, y, i) ∈ RS but that there *does* exist a sequence $y_1, y_2, ..., y_g$ in v such that

$$\text{(i) } y_g = x$$
$$\text{(ii) } y_1 ≠ y$$
$$\text{(iii) } yR_iy_1$$
(iv) for all t, $1 ≤ t ≤ g-1$, either
(a) $y_tP_jy_{t+1}$ for all j ∈ N or
(b) there is a j ≠ i with (y_t, y_{t+1}, j) ∈ RS and $y_tP_jy_{t+1}$.

But suppose also (z, y_1, i) ∈ RS, zP_iy and there do not exist z', S with (z', z, S) ∈ RS. Then if i exercises (x, y, i) he runs a danger that he will be forced down the sequence to y_1 which is no gain over y. But he can repair the damage caused by then exercising (z, y_1, i) which does yield a gain over y and which can not be further damaged. In such a case it isn't right to assume, as Gibbard does, that i will waive (x, y, i).
5. Gibbard's rule works only because people sometimes waive incorrectly. To illustrate this, suppose there are two individuals and X={x, y, z, w}. RS={(x, y, 1), (y, x, 1), (z, w, 2), (w, z, 2)}. Consider profile u:

$$1: wxyz$$
$$2: yzwx.$$

What is $C_u(X)$? If the Pareto condition holds, neither z nor x can be chosen. Under the old automatic rule, #1 would eliminate y and #2 would eliminate w leaving $C_u(X) = ∅$. Gibbard's L'' would have both individuals waive those rights.

Exercise.
175. Prove $(x, y, 1) \in W_1(u, X)$ and $(z, w, 2) \in W_2(u, X)$.

But each has waived on the *incorrect* assumption that the other is following the automatic rule. Each has all the information required to see that the other would not behave in the manner the waiver set definition has him take the other to behave. Who wants to base a libertarian philosophy on the assumption that there is a certain kind of error that all people will repeatedly make in circumstances where they have the requisite information to correct that error?

The last resolution we will examine, one by Kotaro Suzumura, concentrates on rights systems and the presence of an individual who is deferential to others' rights.

Let RS be a rights system. A *critical loop* is a sequence of ordered pairs (x_1, y_1), (x_2, y_2), ..., (x_t, y_t) such that

(i) for each h, $1 \le h \le t$, there is an i such that
$$(x_h, y_h, i) \in RS;$$
(ii) there is not a single i such that $(x_h, y_h, i) \in RS$ for all h;
(iii) for all h, $2 \le h \le t$, $y_{h-1} = x_h$ and also $x_1 = y_t$.

Exercise.
176. Show that the rights system in the wall color example contains a critical loop.

A rights system is *coherent* is if contains no critical loop.

At each profile $u = (R_1, R_2, ..., R_n)$ each individual i specifies a transitive sub-relation R_i^* that i wants "counted" in the collective choice procedure. A social choice rule *realizes* RS if
$(x, y, i) \in RS$ and xP_i^*y implies

$$x \in v \text{ implies } y \notin C_u(v).$$

A social choice rule satisfies the *conditional Pareto condition* if

(i) xR_i^*y for all i implies
$$x \in v\text{-}C_u(v) \text{ implies } y \notin C_u(v);$$
(ii) xP_i^*y for all i implies
$$x \in v \text{ implies } y \notin C_u(v).$$

If RS is coherent, then at any profile u there is at least one ordering on X that subsumes each R_i on i's protected sphere.

Exercise.
177. Prove this last claim.

Let Φ_u be the set of all such orderings. Then individual $j \in N$ is called *deferential* if there is at least one $R \in \Phi_u$ such that
$$R_j^* = R_j \cap R.$$

Theorem (Suzumura). Let RS be a coherent rights system. If there exists at least one deferential individual in the society, then there does exist a social choice rule that satisfies all of

(1) the standard domain constraint;
(2) the conditional Pareto condition;
(3) transitive explanations;

and which realizes RS.

The problem with Suzumura's resolution is obvious if you feel very strongly that there are rights that have to be protected even when no one feels deferential to them. I ought to be able to speak out against what I see as dishonorable political behavior even if everyone else disagrees with me. It should be protected, not just permitted if there happens to be some deferential individual who permits my behavior even though he disagrees with it. There is no protection against everyone else if I need someone else's deference.

Further Reading

Sen's "Liberty, Unanimity and Rights" surveys much of this literature in readable fashion. Harder, but rewarding is Kotaro Suzumura's *Rational Choice, Collective Decisions and Social Welfare* (Cambridge University Press, 1983). This book also contains much on Arrow-type theorems.

Chapter 10. Strategy-Proofness

Let us look again at the staging extension of simple majority voting. With $v = X = \{x, y, z\}$ and three individuals, let xyz be the managing order that determines both the sequence of voting comparisons and the tie-breaking rule. At the true profile u:

$$1: xyz;$$
$$2: yzx;$$
$$3: zxy,$$

we see x beating y in the first stage and then x losing to z at the second stage. Individual #1, seeing her worst alternative chosen, in part because she voted for x at the first stage, considers submitting a false preference order to the social rule. Suppose #2 and #3 continue to submit their true orderings but #1 sends 1: yxz. The social choice rule operates on profile u':

$$1: yxz;$$
$$2: yzx;$$
$$3: zxy.$$

Here y beats x at the first stage and then goes on to beat z at the second stage. Since in #1's true ordering 1: xyz at u, she prefers this outcome, y, to the outcome, z, that results if she tells the truth, we see that for this social choice rule there is a profile at which some individual has an incentive to falsely report preferences. Of course, #1 can only carry out such a calculation if she knows everyone else's preferences as well as details of the rule itself.

Exercises.

178. Show that at profile u, there is no false reporting of preferences by #1 that will enable her to get her most preferred alternative x as the chosen element.

179. Show that at profile u, there is no way for either #2 alone or #3 alone to improve on the outcome by false reporting of preferences.

Suppose two profiles u and u' are i-variants:

$$u = (R_1, R_2, \ldots, R_{i-1}, R_i, R_{i+1}, \ldots, R_n)$$
$$u' = (R_1, R_2, \ldots, R_{i-1}, R_i^*, R_{i+1}, \ldots, R_n)$$

and suppose we consider $C_u(v)$ and $C_{u'}(v)$. If individual i expects agenda v but prefers $C_{u'}(v)$ to $C_u(v)$ *in the R_i ordering*, then, at u, i has an incentive to falsely reveal preferences, to report R_i^* rather than R_i.

Now first notice that individual i, in considering what preference list to submit at u looks only at alternative results at profiles that are i-variants, i.e., although i is considering lying at u, i calculates on the assumption that everyone else will be telling the truth. As one aspect of this, we are only considering the vulnerability of a social choice rule to manipulations by single individuals. We will ignore joint manipulations by coalitions of two or more individuals (but Exercise 180 illustrates *what* we will be ignoring). If it is hard (impossible) to finds social choice rules that satisfy some criteria plus this freedom from *individual* lying, how much harder it would be to get one also free from coalition manipulation.

Exercise.

180. Assume the staging extension based on the order xyz. At the profile

> 1: xyz;
> 2: xyz;
> 3: yzx;
> 4: yzx;
> 5: zxy;
> 6: zxy,

show that neither #1 alone nor #2 alone can alter the outcome by falsely reporting preferences, but they *do* have an incentive to simultaneously lie and both submit yxz.

Next, notice that at our staging example and profile u

> 1: xyz;
> 2: yzx;
> 3: zxy,

whether or not #1 lies depends upon what agenda is involved. We calculated assuming $v = X = \{x, y, z\}$. But if $v = \{x, y\}$, the staging procedure yields $C_u(v) = \{x\}$ and #1 can't hope to gain better than this, her most preferred alternative, by lying. Agenda issues thus are important, but we have no theory to explain how voters form expectations about what agendas will occur after they submit orderings. So we will assume that problem away by working with just a single agenda, the agenda X of all alternatives. We weaken the standard domain constraint so that each choice function C_u need only work at this one agenda of all alternatives. Again, if it is hard (impossible) to satisfy some other criteria plus this weakened domain constraint, how much harder would it be to satisfy also the additional flexibility of the standard domain constraint. Anyway, we will use the *new domain constraint*:

> i) there are at least three alternatives in X;
> ii) there are at least three individuals in N;

iii) the social choice rule has as domain all logically possible profiles of preference orderings on X;

iv) each choice function that is an output of the rule has in its domain the single agenda, X.

Now go back and notice something very strange in our discussion. We asked if in the R_i ordering i preferred $C_{u'}(v)$ to $C_u(v)$. But this generally doesn't make any sense in the informational context we have been assuming. Individuals have preferences over *alternatives*, not over *sets* of alternatives like $C_{u'}(v)$ and $C_u(v)$. Suppose $v = \{x, y, z\}$; that at u we have

$$i: xyz;$$

and $C_u(v)=\{x, z\}$ and $C_{u'}(v)=\{y\}$. We have no way to know from R_i alone how i would choose between a set of just y and a set that contains one better and one worse alternative. We will again assume the problem away, this time by working in a context where outcomes are always singletons. Rules that give choice functions that always choose singletons are called *resolute.* Now it is still not quite correct, when we have at u

$$i: xyz$$

and $C_{u'}(v)=\{x\}$ and $C_u(v)=\{y\}$, to say i prefers $C_{u'}(v)$ to $C_u(v)$. A singleton set is a different thing from its one member ($1 \in \{1\}$ but $1 \notin 1$). We would more accurately say i prefers the member of $C_{u'}(v)$ to the member of $C_u(v)$. But this is overly fussy and we will sometime abuse our language and notation; for a resolute rule we will not always distinguish between $C_u(v)$ and its one member. This allows us to write not only something like $C_u(v) \in v$ but also something like $C_{u'}(v)P_iC_u(v)$. This allows us to frame the following definitions for resolute rules. A rule is *manipulable* by i at u and v if there is an i-variant profile u' with $C_{u'}(v)P_iC_u(v)$ where R_i is i's ordering *at u*. A rule is *strategy-proof* if there is no possible choice of i, u and v such that the rule is manipulable by i at u and v. Clearly, manipulability calculations by i require either luck or knowledge of u and of the rule.

We are interested in strategy-proof rules for five main reasons[1].

1. Manipulation introduces an element of randomness into collective decisions.
2. Unequal manipulative skills may lead to destruction of our efforts to design rules with equal treatments of individuals.
3. Voters are led to waste resources in manipulation calculations.
4. We are led to try to reduce manipulation of others against us by concealing our preferences, reducing a flow of information that might aid in collective decision making.
5. Manipulation by representatives blurs their voting record and makes it difficult for us to determine if they are really representing our interests.

How hard is it to find strategy-proof resolute social choice rules satisfying the new domain constraint? Not hard at all, as the next four exercises show.

---

[1] See Mark Satterthwaite's *The Existence of a Strategy Proof Voting Procedure* (PhD Dissertation, University of Wisconsin, 1973).

Exercises.

181. Let $x \in X$ and consider the rule $const_x$ defined by $C_u(X) = \{x\}$ for all u. Show that this rule is resolute, strategy-proof and satisfies the new domain constraint.

182. Let $X = \{x_1, x_2, x_3, \dots\}$ and consider the rule f that chooses the lowest labeled alternative in #1's topmost indifference set.)

$$C_u(X) = \{x_t\} \text{ where } x_t R_1 x_s \text{ for all } x_s \in X \text{ and}$$
$$t \leq s \text{ for all } x_s \text{ such that } x_s R_1 x_t.$$

Show that this rule is resolute, strategy-proof and satisfies the new domain constraint.

183. Let $x, y \in X$ and consider the rule defined by

$$C_u(X) = \begin{cases} x \text{ if at u every one strictly prefers x to y;} \\ \\ y \text{ otherwise.} \end{cases}$$

Show that this rule is resolute, strategy-proof and satisfies the new domain constraint.

184. Let $x, y \in X$ and consider the rule defined by

$$C_u(X) = \begin{cases} x \text{ if } N(x R_i y) \geq N(y R_i x) \text{ at u} \\ \\ y \text{ otherwise} \end{cases}$$

(This is majority voting between x and y with ties broken in favor of x.) Show that this rule is resolute, strategy-proof and satisfies the standard domain constraint.

Of course, these rules are just terrible. The rule in Exercise 182 has a dictator; $\{1\}$ is a decisive set. The choice rules in Exercises 181, 183 and 184 have very reduced ranges. In the rule of Exercise 181, as we allow u to vary, there is only one alternative, x, that is ever chosen. Remember the domain constraint tells us X has at least three alternatives. All but one of these are never chosen. Even at a profile where everyone unanimously agrees that x is their least preferred alternative, x is still chosen. The rules of Exercises 183 and 184 are only slightly better – only two alternatives are ever chosen. There are some alternatives that are never chosen, not even when they are at the top of everyone's ordering.

For the decisiveness problem of Exercise 182, we have a simple recourse; we shall require a social choice rule to have no dictator. For the reduced range problem of Exercises 181, 183 and 184, we could try several things. We might invoke a Pareto condition or, somewhat weaker, require that each alternative in X be chosen at some profile. It will be sufficient for our purposes to work with the even weaker requirement we call the *range constraint:*

> there are at least three alternatives in X
> each of which has the property that it is
> chosen at some profile u.

Define

$$X_f = \{x \in X \ / \ C_u(X) = \{x\} \text{ for some } u\};$$

then the range constraint is simply that X_f contains at least three members.

Can we find a strategy-proof resolute social choice rule with no dictator satisfying both the new domain constraint and the range constraint? This is a *much* harder problem. Let us illustrate the difficulties by considering a slightly simpler problem; we will alter the new domain constraint so that there are only two individuals and the social choice rule only has to work where everyone's preferences are strong. We can examine such rules by means of tables like the one in

	x y z	x z y	y x z	y z x	z x y	z y x
xyz						
xzy			y			
yxz						
yzx						
zxy						
zyx						

Figure 10-1.

Figure 10-1. Here each box represents a profile. On the left are preferences for #1; at top are preferences for #2. For example, the box in the second row, third column (where a y appears) is the profile u:

1: xzy;
2: yxz.

The entry in the box is the (unique) element chosen from the one agenda, X, at that profile; $C_u(X) = \{y\}$.

Thus we can describe a resolute social choice rule defined at agenda X at every profile of strong preferences by putting one symbol in each box. For example, consider the rule of Exercise 184 (now thought of as working for just two individuals each with only strong orders). This would appear as shown in Figure 10-2. To examine manipulability in these tables, you must see that the 1-variants of any profile (box) are the boxes in the same column while the 2-variants are the boxes in the same row. Thus to see if a rule is manipulable by #1 at a profile, you need

	x y z	x z y	y x z	y z x	z x y	z y x
xyz	x	x	x	x	x	x
xzy	x	x	x	x	x	x
yxz	x	x	y	y	x	y
yzx	x	x	y	y	x	y
zxy	x	x	x	x	x	x
zyx	x	x	y	y	x	x

Figure 10-2.

only look to see if there is a better outcome in the same column. To see if it is manipulable by #2, you need only see if there is an outcome in the same row better for #2. For example, look at Figure 10-3 which shows just part of a social choice rule. Focus on the profile u in row four, column four (where the x appears). This rule is

	x y z	x z y	y x z	y z x	z x y	z y x
xyz						
xzy						
yxz						
yzx				x	y	
zxy						
zyx				z		

Figure 10-3.

manipulable by #1 at this profile, because there is a 1-variant profile u′ (i.e., a profile in the same column) which yields an outcome, z, which #1 prefers according to her ordering at u. (z is also preferred to x by #1 at the new profile u′, but that is not relevant to manipulability at u.) In fact, at u, this rule is also manipulable by #2, because there is a 2-variant profile, u″ (i.e., a profile in the same row which yields an outcome, y, which he prefers according to his ordering at u. (This time y is *not* preferred to x by #2 at the new profile, u″, but still that is not relevant to manipulability at u.)

Exercise.
185. Do you have enough information to decide if this rule is manipulable at u′? At u″?

Now let's examine manipulability for a fully described rule. In Figure 10–4 we have a representation for the rule defined by

$C_u(X) = z$ if z is at the top of #2's order; otherwise, $C_u(X)$ is whatever is at the top of #1's ordering.

This rule is clearly resolute, is defined at every profile and satisfies the range constraint (all three alternatives appear in one box or another). Also the rule has no dictator (#1 doesn't always

	x y z	x z y	y x z	y z x	z x y	z y x
xyz	x	x	x	x	z	z
xzy	x	x	x	x	z	z
yxz	y	y	y	y	z	z
yzx	y	y	y	y	z	z
zxy	z	z	z	z	z	z
zyx	z	z	z	z	z	z

Figure 10–4.

get x in row one; #2 doesn't always get x in column one). Is it strategy-proof? We must first see if it is manipulable by #1, then if it is manipulable by #2. To see if it is manipulable by #1, we must check each of the 36 boxes to see if #1 can do better at a 1-variant (i.e., in the same column). But this is easy. If we are anywhere in the last two columns, #1 *can't* influence the outcome; if we are in the first four columns, #1 *can* influence the outcome but *isn't willing to.* She's already getting her most preferred outcome.

What about manipulability by #2? Again we must check each of the 36 boxes to see if #2 can do better at a 2-variant (i.e., in the same row). If we are anywhere in the last two rows, #2 *can't* influence the outcome. If we are anywhere in the last two columns, #2 certainly isn't willing to; in those boxes, #2 is already getting his most preferred outcome. So we need only look at the 16 boxes in the first four rows and four columns. At any of those profiles, the only thing #2 can do is force a change to z by reporting a preference with z at the top. So this rule is manipulable at one of those 16 profiles only if there #2 prefers z to the outcome. In the first three boxes of the first row, the outcome is x and at each of those profiles #2 prefers x to z hence is not willing to alter the outcome. But at row one, column four #2 prefers z to the outcome x there and is able to force z. Thus this rule is manipulable by #2 at the profile in row one, column four.

Exercises.

186. Show that the rule in Figure 10-4 is also manipulable by #2 at the profiles located at

    i) row two, column four;
    ii) row three, column two;
    iii) row four, column two.

187. In Figure 10-5 is a representation of the rule that gives the alphabetically earliest of the Pareto optimal alternatives (check that this is correct). Check that this rule has no dictator and that the range constraint is satisfied. Find the four profiles at which this rule is manipulable.

	x y z	x z y	y x z	y z x	z x y	z y x
xyz	x	x	x	x	x	x
xzy	x	x	x	x	x	x
yxz	x	x	y	y	x	y
yzx	x	x	y	y	y	y
zxy	x	x	x	y	z	z
zyx	x	x	y	y	z	z

Figure 10-5.

188. In Figure 10-6 is a representation of the rule that gives the alphabetically earliest of the alternatives with the lowest global Borda count
(check that this is correct). Check that this rule has no dictator and that
the range constraint is satisfied. Find the 14 profiles at which this rule is
manipulable.

	x y z	x z y	y x z	y z x	z x y	z y x
xyz	x	x	x	y	x	x
xzy	x	x	x	x	x	z
yxz	x	x	y	y	x	y
yzx	y	x	y	y	z	y
zxy	x	x	x	z	z	z
zyx	x	z	y	y	z	z

Figure 10-6.

These exercises suggest that we are having trouble finding a strategy-proof resolute rule unless we have a dictator or unless we have fewer than three alternatives
in the range. Let's deal with that more systematically. First we'll see that if the rule
satisfies the range constraint and strategy-proofness then at any profile where an
alternative is at the top of *both* orderings, that alternative must be chosen. This will
determine one third of such a rule. Without a lot of rigor, we illustrate the derivation in Figure 10-7. We want to show, for example, that an x must appear in the
upper left corner box where x is at the top of both lists (s. Fig. 10-7). By the range
constraint, x must appear *somewhere* in the table. For illustration, we have assumed an x appears in row four, column five, but it doesn't really make any difference where this "seed" entry of x is located. Now stay in the same row but come
all the way back to the first column. Our claim is that in this new box (row four,
column one) an x must appear; otherwise the rule would be manipulable at this
new box by #2 who would otherwise force his most preferred x by moving right
along the fourth row. Now that we know x appears at row four, column one, come
back up to row one, column one. Again, our claim is that in this last box an x must
appear; otherwise the rule would be manipulable here by #1 who would otherwise force her most preferred x by moving down the first column.

This derivation that x appears in row one, column one will (s. Fig. 10-8) work

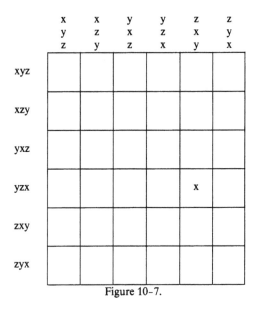

	x y z	x z y	y x z	y z x	z x y	z y x
xyz						
xzy						
yxz						
yzx					x	
zxy						
zyx						

Figure 10-7.

	x y z	x z y	y x z	y z x	z x y	z y x
xyz	x	x				
xzy	x	x				
yxz			y	y		
yzx			y	y		
zxy					z	z
zyx					z	z

Figure 10-8.

for any box in which x is at the top in both orderings and regardless of where the first x "seed" is located. A similar derivation will put y in any box where y is at the top in both orderings; similarly for z. These analyses provide us, in Figure 10-8, with a partial representation of any strategy-proof resolute rule satisfying the range constraint.

	x y z	x z y	y x z	y z x	z x y	z y x
xyz	x	x	-z			
xzy	x	x				
yxz			y	y		
yzx			y	y		
zxy					z	z
zyx					z	z

Figure 10-9.

But there is more we can learn about the representation of any strategy-proof resolute rule that starts like Figure 10-8. Look in the box in row one, column three of that table. Suppose z occurred there. Then #2 would force a move to the left and gain the preferred x; the rule would be manipulable at row one, column three. If the rule is to be strategy-proof, z can not appear in that position. This is indicated in Figure 10-9 by a "-z" (read "not z") in that box. Similar analyses can be made anywhere in rows one and

	x y z	x z y	y x z	y z x	z x y	z y x
xyz	x	x -z			-y	
xzy	x	x -z			-y	
yxz	-z		y	y		-x
yzx	-z		y	y		-x
zxy		-y		-x	z	z
zyx		-y		-x	z	z

Figure 10-10.

two for any alternative #2 considers worse than x. Then the same can be done in rows three and four for any alternative #2 considers worse than y; and in rows five and six for any alternatives he considers worse than z. All this information is included in Figure 10-10. Finally, similar analyses based on the possibility of manipulation by #1 will rule out additional possibilities; the results are given in Figure 10-11.

Exercise.
189. Confirm each of these entries in Figures 10-10 and 10-11.

---

	x y z	x z y	y x z	y z x	z x y	z y x
xyz	x	x	-z	-z	-y	
xzy	x	x	-z		-y	-y
yxz	-z	-z	y	y		-x
yzx	-z		y	y	-x	-x
zxy	-y	-y		-x	z	z
zyx		-y	-x	-x	z	z

Figure 10-11.

Now let's start from Figure 10-11 and try a different approach. Look at the upper right hand corner where #1 and #2 completely disagree; their orderings are mirror images of one another. So far we have learned nothing about rule outcomes at this location. Each of the other five locations where we have no information also represent cases where #1 and #2 completely disagree; #2's ordering is the exact opposite of #1's. For these cases, there is a common alternative in the middle of both orderings; in the upper right corner this middle alternative is y. We will show that if y is the outcome at that corner, there will be a manipulation, a violation of strategy-proofness. The same kind of analysis would then allow us to rule out the choice of the middle alternative at each of the other five mirror image locations.

So suppose y *is* chosen in the upper right corner (see Figure 10-12). Since y is in row one, column six, we can't have z in row one, column five or the rule will be manipulable at the corner profile.

	x y z	x z y	y x z	y z x	z x y	z y x
xyz	x	x	-z	-z	-y	y
xzy	x	x	-z		-y	-y
yxz	-z	-z	y	y		-x
yzx	-z		y	y	-x	-x
zxy	-y	-y		-x	z	z
zyx		-y	-x	-x	z	z

Figure 10-12.

But already we know y isn't chosen in row one, column five, so that box must have x. Since x appears there, it must also appear in the box just below that (where otherwise we would have manipulability by #1). But an x in row two, column five means z can't appear in row two, column six or the rule would be manipulable by #2 at row two, column five. Since already we had y not in row two, column six we must have an x there. But an x there and a y just above it means the rule is manipulable by #1 at row one, column six. There is *no* strategy-proof resolute rule whatsoever starting from Figure 10-12.

	x y z	x z y	y x z	y z x	z x y	z y x
xyz	x	x	-z	-z	-y	-y
xzy	x	x	-z	-z	-y	-y
yxz	-z	-z	y	y	-x	-x
yzx	-z	-z	y	y	-x	-x
zxy	-y	-y	-x	-x	z	z
zyx	-y	-y	-x	-x	z	z

Figure 10-13.

Thus we can put "-y" in the upper right corner. Analogously, we can take each of the other empty boxes in Figure 10-11 and indicate that the middle alternative can't occur there. The result is Figure 10-13.

Now we will return to that upper right corner with its new "-y". Either x or z must appear there; suppose for the moment the entry here is x. We will show that this entails #1's dictatorship. A similar analysis would show that a z in the corner would entail #2's dictatorship.

With an x in the upper right corner, the whole first row must be x's or #2 will manipulate to the left from the corner (put x's all along row one in Figure 10-13). Then the whole second row (where x is #1's best) must also be all x's or #1 will manipulate up to the first row from there. Figure 10-14 shows what results.

	x y z	x z y	y x z	y z x	z x y	z y x
xyz	x	x	x	x	x	x
xzy	x	x	x	x	x	x
yxz	-z	-z	y	y	-x	-x
yzx	-z	-z	y	y	-x	-x
zxy	-y	-y	-x	-x	z	z
zyx	-y	-y	-x	-x	z	z

Figure 10-14.

Now, as once before, we can rule out some possible outcomes. Since x's appear in row one, #1's potential manipulations rule out any alternative being chosen anywhere that it is ranked worse than x by her. For example, we could get -z everywhere in row three. Since in the fifth box of row three we already have -x, this tells us y must appear there. Similarly y is ruled out in row five. All this information appears in Figure 10-15.

Examining Figure 10-15, we then see the y that must appear in row three, column five is #2's worst. Strategy-proofness then requires y throughout row three. Since y's fill the third row, they must also fill the fourth or #1 would manipulate from the fourth row to the third. Exercise 190 has us continue this analysis and show that the last two rows must be all z's (see Figure 10-16).

Exercise.
190. Derive the rest of the steps leading from Figure 10-15 to Figure 10-16.

	x y z	x z y	y x z	y z x	z x y	z y x
xyz	x	x	x	x	x	x
xzy	x	x	x	x	x	x
yxz	-z	-z	y	y	y -x, -z	y -x, -z
yzx	-z	-z	y	y	-x	-x
zxy	-y	-y	z -x, -y	z -x, -y	z	z
zyx	-y	-y	-x	-x	z	z

Figure 10-15.

	x y z	x z y	y x z	y z x	z x y	z y x
xyz	x	x	x	x	x	x
xzy	x	x	x	x	x	x
yxz	y	y	y	y	y	y
yzx	y	y	y	y	y	y
zxy	z	z	z	z	z	z
zyx	z	z	z	z	z	z

Figure 10-16.

Let us summarize what we have derived so far. If our social choice rule is strategy-proof, resolute, satisfies the range constraint and works at every profile, then:

if x appears in the upper right corner, we get
the rule in Figure 10-16, where #1 is a dictator.

116

Symmetrically,

> if z appears in the upper right corner, we get
> the rule in Figure 10-17, where #2 is a dictator.

Exercise.
191. Obtain this last result by the same kind of box-by-box analysis from
Figure 10-11 that we used in deriving Figure 10-16.

---

	x y z	x z y	y x z	y z x	z x y	z y x
xyz	x	x	y	y	z	z
xzy	x	x	y	y	z	z
yxz	x	x	y	y	z	z
yzx	x	x	y	y	z	z
zxy	x	x	y	y	z	z
zyx	x	x	y	y	z	z

Figure 10-17.

If we seek a strategy-proof resolute social choice rule defined on all pairs of strong orderings and satisfying the range constraint, it can *only* be one of two rules: the one in Figure 10-16, wholly determined by the dictatorship of #1, or the one in Figure 10-17, wholly determined by the dictatorship of #2. Put differently, with three alternatives, two individuals and only strong orders, there *does not exist* a strategy-proof, resolute social choice rule satisfying the range constraint and a no dictatorship condition.

Of course, this is a very narrow result, depending as it does on the assumptions of three alternatives, two individuals and strong preference orderings. But none of this is crucial. In one of the important recent developments in social choice theory, Allan Gibbard and Mark Satterthwaite learned that our result can be extended to a vastly more general setting.

Theorem (Gibbard-Satterthwaite[2]). There does not exist any social choice rule satisfying all of

---

[2] Gibbard, Allan, "Manipulation of Voting Schemes: A General Result, " *Econometrica* Vol. 41, No. 4 (July, 1973), pp. 587-601.
Satterthwaite, Mark A., "Strategy-proofness and Arrow's Conditions, " *Journal of Economic Theory* Vol. 10, No. 2 (April, 1975), 187-217.

1) the new domain constraint;
2) the range constraint;
3) resoluteness;
4) no dictator;
5) strategy-proofness.

Exercises.

192. We saw back in Chapter 3 that restricting admissible preferences (e.g., single-peakedness) allows one to circumvent some problems of voting rules. Similarly, restricting preferences can allow us to circumvent manipulability problems. In the following diagram, suppose no one can have preference ordering zxy and so also that zxy is not an admissible ordering to submit to the social choice rule.

	x y z	x z y	y x z	y z x	z y x
xyz					
xzy					
yxz					
yzx					
zyx					

Figure 10–18.

Show that this table *can* be filled in so that all three alternatives appear, neither player is a dictator and no manipulability occurs.

193. In the previous exercise we assumed that both individuals were precluded from submitting the same ordering; this is not crucial. Fill in the following table (where #1 can not have zyx and #2 can not have zxy) so that all three alternatives appear, neither player is a dictator and no manipulability occurs.

	x y z	x z y	y x z	y z x	z y x
xyz					
xzy					
yxz					
yzx					
zxy					

Figure 10-19.

Further Reading

The box diagrams were first used for exposition of the Gibbard-Satterthwaite ideas in Allan M. Feldman's *Welfare Economics and Social Choice Theory* (Nijhoff, 1980) which integrates the social choice work we have been examining with traditional economic analysis of public goods provision. Prasanta Pattanaik's *Strategy and Group Choice* (North-Holland, 1978) expands on much of the material in this chapter including dropping the requirement of resoluteness. My favorite proof of the Gibbard-Satterthwaite theorem derives that result from Arrow's impossibility theorem; see David Schmeidler and Hugo Sonnenschein's "Two proofs of the Gibbard-Satterthwaite Theorem on the Possibility of a Strategy-Proof Social Choice Function, " in *Decision Theory and Social Ethics* (Reidel, 1978) edited by Hans W. Gottinger and Werner Leinfellner.

Chapter 11. Counterthreats

In this chapter, we take up the first of two responses to the Gibbard-Satterthwaite theorem on the impossibility of designing strategy-proof rules. This first response, due to Prasanta Pattanaik, makes strategy-proofness easier by showing why manipulation won't take place at some profiles where we would have expected it in the last chapter. The second response is to recognize that *some* lying will take place and then try to design rules that reduce (but not to zero!) the amount of manipulation. This second response will be taken up in the next chapter.

Consider Figure 11–1, where we have the representation of the rule that gives #2's top ranked alternative *unless* #2 has the order xzy and #1 has the order yzx, in which case #1's best, y, is chosen.

	x y z	x z y	y x z	y z x	z x y	z y x
xyz	x	x	y	y	z	z
xzy	x	x	y	y	z	z
yxz	x	x	y	y	z	z
yzx	x	y	y	y	z	z
zxy	x	x	y	y	z	z
zyx	x	x	y	y	z	z

Figure 11–1.

At profile u in row three, column two, where an x appears, we would say this rule is manipulable by #1 because, by reporting yzx and moving down column two to the box in row four, #1 could obtain y which she prefers at the original profile. But suppose, back at u, #2 announces to #1 that if she reports yzx then he, #2, will report zxy. This will put us in row four, column five where the chosen element is z. There are two things to say about #2's proposed counter move to #1's threat of manipulation; these two remarks play a central role in the main definitions of this chapter:

i) #2's counter move yields an outcome, z, that, at u, #1 considers worse than the result, x, that results if she doesn't manipulate in the first place. Thus #1 really sees #2's counter move as a counter *threat*.

ii) #1 would see #2's counterthreat as *credible* since, at u, #2 doesn't like the outcome, y, of #1's manipulation as much as the original outcome, x, *and* #2 prefers the outcome, z, that results from carrying out the counterthreat to y which results if #1 manipulates and #2 does nothing.

Pattanaik suggests that in these circumstances, it is not serious that the rule is manipulable by #1 at row three, column two, because #1 would not actually carry out that manipulation, being deterred by her expectation that #2 would carry out his credible counterthreat that would leave #1 with an alternative worse than what results when she chooses not to manipulate in the first place.

Now to our main definitions. As in the last chapter, a rule is *manipulable* by individual i at profile $u = (R_1, R_2, ..., R_n)$ if there exists an i-variant profile $u' = (R_1', R_2', ..., R_n')$ such that

$$C_{u'}(X)P_iC_u(X).$$

Let S be a coalition of other individuals, $i \notin S \subset N$; this coalition has a *counterthreat* to i's manipulation at u if there is a profile $u'' = (R_1'', R_2'', ..., R_n'')$ that differs from u' only for members of S

$$k \notin S \text{ implies } R_k'' = R_k'$$

and such that

$$C_u(X)P_iC_{u''}(X).$$

Thus a counterthreat is a move by S to u'' from i's manipulation to u' that will make i worse off than if things were left at the original profile, u. If i has a manipulation from u to u' and S has a counterthreat from u' to u'', we call that counterthreat *credible* if, for all $j \in S$,

$$C_u(X)P_jC_{u'}(X) \text{ and } C_{u''}(X)P_jC_{u'}(X).$$

A rule is *strategy-proof by counterthreats* if for every profile u and individual i such that the rule is manipulable at u by i, there is a coalition that has a credible counterthreat.

Exercises.

194. If S has a counterthreat to i and $S \subset S^*$ where $i \notin S^*$, then S^* also has a counterthreat to i. If S^*'s counterthreat is credible, so is S's, but the converse is not true.

195. Show that the rule represented in Figure 11–1 is manipulable by #1 at row six, column two but that, again, #2 has a credible counterthreat. Show that this rule is manipulable by #2 at row four, column two, but that this time #1 has no counterthreat.

Exercise 195 is very important. It illustrates the idea that although some potential manipulations may be eliminated by permitting counterthreats, it may be difficult to design a good social choice rule in which counterthreats eliminate *all* possible manipulations. Of course, if we don't require *anything else* of a rule, we can easily find some that are strategy-proof by counterthreats. E.g., note that if a rule is strategy-proof then it is strategy-proof by counterthreats. Hence each of the following rules are strategy-proof by counterthreats in the three alternative, two individual strong order context:

i) the rule, $const_x$, which selects x at every profile;
ii) the dictatorial rule which always selects the alternative at the top of #1's preference ordering;
iii) the rule that never selects z, choosing between x and y by simple majority votes (ties broken in favor of x).

Can we find rules that are *not* (ordinary) strategy-proof but *are* strategy-proof by counterthreats? Let's try some.

Exercises.

196. Figure 11–2 is a representation of the rule that selects the alphabetically earliest of the Pareto optimal

	x y z	x z y	y x z	y z x	z x y	z y x
xyz	x	x	x	x	x	x
xzy	x	x	x	x	x	x
yxz	x	x	y	y	x	y
yzx	x	x	y	y	y	y
zxy	x	x	x	y	z	z
zyx	x	x	y	y	z	z

Figure 11–2.

alternatives. You confirmed this in Exercise 187 where you saw that this rule was resolute, free of dictators and satisfied the range constraint.This rule is manipulable by #1 at

1) row three, column five;
2) row five, column four and is manipulable by #2 at
3) row four, column five;
4) row six, column three.

Show that for *none* of these possible manipulations is there a counterthreat.

197. Figure 11-3 is a representation of the rule that gives the alphabetically earliest of the alternatives with lowest global Borda count. In Exercise 188 we learned that this resolute, dictator-free rule which satisfies the range constraint is

	x y z	x z y	y x z	y z x	z x y	z y x
xyz	x	x	x	y	x	x
xzy	x	x	x	x	x	z
yxz	x	x	y	y	x	y
yzx	y	x	y	y	z	y
zxy	x	x	x	z	z	z
zyx	x	z	y	y	z	z

Figure 11-3.

manipulable at 14 different combinations of profile and individual.

Show that

1) at row two, column six, the rule is manipulable by #1, but that #2 has a credible counterthreat.
2) at row six, column four, the rule is manipulable by #2; #1 has a counterthreat, but none that is credible.
3) at row six, column one, the rule is manipulable by #1 and #2 has no counterthreat at all.

198. Figure 11-4 is a representation of the staging extension of simple majority voting when the ordering xyz determines both the sequence of votes and tie breaking.

	x y z	x z y	y x z	y z x	z x y	z y x
xyz	x	x	x	x	x	x
xzy	x	x	x	x	x	x
yxz	x	x	y	y	x	y
yzx	x	x	y	y	z	y
zxy	x	x	x	z	z	z
zyx	x	x	y	y	z	z

Figure 11-4.

Find a profile at which this rule is manipulable by individual # 1 and where # 2 does not have a credible counterthreat.

Motivated by these exercises, we seek to show that in the three alternative, two individual strong order context, that allowing counterthreats doesn't help enough. In this context, given *any* non-dictatorial resolute rule defined at all strong profiles and satisfying the range constraint there will be at least one manipulation for which there is no credible counterthreat. The only rules that are strategy-proof with counterthreats are the strategy-proof rules.

Basically, we will use the same diagram approach we developed in Chapter 10. But we will reduce the amount of detail work by proving the

Intermediate Result. Suppose there are two individuals and three alternatives and we have a resolute social choice rule that

1) works on all profiles $u = (P_1, P_2)$ of strong orders;
2) yields choice functions C_u that work at the one
   agenda, X;
3) has $X = X_f$, i.e., all three alternatives are outcomes
   at some profile or other; and
4) is strategy-proof by counterthreats.

Suppose X can be partitioned into two disjoint sets A and B (= X - A) such that

i) A is not empty and
ii) at $u = (P_1, P_2)$, both individuals strictly prefer everything in A to everything in B.
   Then $C_u(X) \in A$.

Before we prove the Intermediate Result, let's make several observations about it. First, we only show it works for three alternatives and two individuals; this is not an easy result to extend beyond these limitations. Second, it does *not* imply a Pareto condition. At a profile like

$$1: xzy;$$
$$2: yxz,$$

everyone prefers x to z but we can't use the Intermediate Result to say z won't be chosen since there is no proper subset B of X

	x y z	x z y	y x z	y z x	z x y	z y x
xyz	x	x				
xzy	x	x				
yxz			y	y		
yzx			y	y		
zxy					z	z
zyx					z	z

Figure 11–5.

containing z such that everyone prefers everything outside B to everything in B. Third, the Intermediate Result does provide a great deal of information about constructing the diagram for a social choice rule that is strategy-proof by counterthreats. Suppose at u some alternative, say y, is at the *top* of everyone's order. Take $A = \{y\}$, $B = X - \{y\}$. Assuming the range constraint is satisfied, we can use the Intermediate Result to conclude $C_u(X) = y$. This would allow us to determine that our diagram must start like Figure 11–5 (Compare with Figure 10–8).

Even more can be done. Suppose at u some alternative, say y, is at the *bottom* of everyone's order; take $A = X - \{y\}$ and $B = \{y\}$. Then use the Intermediate Result to get $C_u(X) \in A$, i.e., $C_u(X) \neq y$. This allows us to put -y in such a box. Additions of this sort are incorporated in Figure 11–6.

Now that we see the power of this result, let's turn to a proof:

Proof of the Intermediate Result. Suppose at profile $u = (P_1, P_2)$ there are sets A and B satisfying i) and ii) but that $C_u(X) \in B$. We wish to obtain a contradiction.

	x y z	x z y	y x z	y z x	z x y	z y x
xyz	x	x	-z			
xzy	x	x		·	-y	
yxz	-z		y	y		
yzx			y	y		-x
zxy		-y			z	z
zyx				-x	z	z

Figure 11-6.

By i) and the range constraint, there is a profile $u' = (P_1', P_2')$ such that $C_{u'}(X) \in$ A. Consider the three profile sequence

$$u1 = (P_1, P_2) = u \text{ with } C_{u1}(X) \in B$$
$$u2 = (P_1', P_2)$$
$$u3 = (P_1', P_2') = u' \text{ with } C_{u3}(X) \in A.$$

Case 1. $C_{u2}(X) \in A$.
Then, since #1 prefers $C_{u2}(X)$ to $C_{u1}(X)$ at u1, the rule is manipulable by #1 at u1. Can the only possible coalition, {2}, pose a credible counterthreat? Suppose {2} threatens to move from u2 to $u'' = (P_1', P_2^*)$. For this to be a counterthreat it must hurt #1:

$$C_u(X) \, P_1 C_{u''}(X).$$

But since $C_u(X) \in B$ and P_1 ranks all of A above all of B this must entail $C_{u''}(X) \in B$. But then #2's counterthreat isn't credible since, at u1, #2 prefers $C_{u2}(X)$ ($\in$ A) to $C_{u''}(X)$ ($\in$ B).
Case 2. $C_{u2}(X) \in B$.
Since #2 prefers $C_{u3}(X)$ to $C_{u2}(X)$ at u2, the rule is manipulable by #2 at u2. Can {1} pose a credible counterthreat? Suppose {1} threatens to move from u3 to $u'' = (P_1^*, P_2')$. For this to be a counterthreat it must hurt #2:

$$C_{u2}(X) P_2 C_{u''}(X).$$

But since $C_{u2}(X) \in B$ and P_2 ranks all of A above all of B, this must entail $C_{u''}(X) \in B$. For #1's counterthreat to be credible, we need at u2

$$C_{u2}(X) P_1' C_{u3}(X) \text{ and}$$
$$C_{u''}(X) P_1' C_{u3}(X).$$

But *now* we have shown that this rule is manipulable by #1 at u3 and since $C_{u3}(X)$ is at the *bottom* of P_1' at u3, there is *no* counterthreat to this manipulation and we have a contradiction of strategy-proofness by counterthreats. ∎

The last step of this proof exploits the idea that there can't be counterthreats to individual manipulations away from worst alternatives. This idea allows us to improve on Figure 11–6, where, for example, in row one, column five we can't have a y or else #2 would manipulate away from this worst alternative to gain an x in column one. Figure 11–7 includes the additional information based on this approach. (Compare this diagram with Figure 10–11.)

	x y z	x z y	y x z	y z x	z x y	z y x
xyz	x	x	-z	-z	-y	
xzy	x	x	-z		-y	-y
yxz	-z	-z	y	y		-x
yzx	-z		y	y	-x	-x
zxy	-y	-y		-x	z	z
zyx		-y	-x	-x	z	z

Figure 11–7.

Exercise.
199. Confirm all the new entries in Figure 11–7.

Now, as in Chapter 10, we will focus on the box in the upper right corner where #1 and #2 are diametrically opposed. We wish to show first that if y appears there then a violation of strategy-proofness by counterthreats must occur; if x appears there then #1 must be a dictator; if z, then #2 must be a dictator.

So let's start by putting a y in the upper right corner and then look for a manipulation for which there is no credible counterthreat. With a y in the upper right corner, we can exploit again the idea that manipulations away from bottom-ranked alternatives can't be blocked by counterthreats. So, for example, a y in row one, column six, means z can't appear in the box at row three, column six or #1 would manipulate away from that box to the corner. Since at row three, column six we already had -x, adding -z means y appears there. Figure 11–8 shows this result together with another entry based on the same kind of argument.

Focus on the box in row three, column five of Figure 11-8. We want to show that each possible entry there creates a violation of strategy-proofness by counterthreats.

Case 1. Row three, column five has z.

Since z is #1's worst, #1 would manipulate *without counterthreats* to anything else. So strategy-proofness by counterthreats requires that all of column five is z. But then at row three, column six, #2 would manipulate left one box and #1 has no counterthreat.

	x y z	x z y	y x z	y z x	z x y	z y x
xyz	x	x	-z	y -z, -x	-y	y
xzy	x	x	-z		-y	-y
yxz	-z	-z	y	y		y -x, -z
yzx	-z		y	y	-x	-x
zxy	-y	-y		-x	z	z
zyx		-y	-x	-x	z	z

Figure 11-8.

Case 2. Row three, column five has either x or y.

Then there can't be a z in row one, column five or #1 could move away from his worst. Hence there is an x in row one, column five. Now there can't be a z in row two, column five because then #1 would move from there to row one, column five and the only possible counterthreat (y) wouldn't be credible since y is #2's least preferred. Hence there is an x in row two, column five. Now there can't be a z in row two, column six because then #2 could move there from row two, column five and the only possible counterthreat (y) wouldn't be credible since y is #1's least preferred. Hence there is an x in row two, column six. Since, there, x is #1's least preferred, there must be x's all across row two. But then #1 could manipulate from row one, column six to row two, column six and there is no possible counterthreat.

At this point, we know that the entry in the upper right corner can *not* be y. We will demonstrate that if the entry is x then #1 is a dictator. Our analysis will be completed by Exercise 200.

> *Exercise.*
> 200. While working through the next few paragraphs, develop the analogous argument, starting from z in the upper right box, to show that then #2 is a dictator.

Since in the upper right corner x is #2's worst, all of row one must be x's. Then also all of row two must be x's or else #1 will manipulate up to row one where there is no possibility of a counterthreat. We are at the position in Figure 11-9.

	x y z	x z y	y x z	y z x	z x y	z y x
xyz	x	x	x	x	x	x
xzy	x	x	x	x	x	x
yxz	-z	-z	y	y		-x
yzx	-z		y	y	-x	-x
zxy	-y	-y		-x	z	z
zyx		-y	-x	-x	z	z

Figure 11-9.

Since at row three, column six z is #1's worst, we have -z there. Since already -x, there must be a y in that box. Now if there were a z in row four, column six, #1 could manipulate to that box from the y at row three, column six. The only possible counterthreat is to x, but that is #2's worst so the threat wouldn't be credible. So there isn't a z there and y must appear in that box. Next if there were a z at row four, column five, #2 would manipulate there from column six; since both like x least there, no credible counterthreat exists. Thus y is chosen here in row four, column five where y is #2's worst. So all of row four must be y. All of row three then must also be y or else #1 would manipulate to row four where no possible counterthreat exists. We are at the position in Figure 11-10.

	x y z	x z y	y x z	y z x	z x y	z y x
xyz	x	x	x	x	x	x
xzy	x	x	x	x	x	x
yxz	y	y	y	y	y	y
yzx	y	y	y	y	y	y
zxy					z	z
	-y	-y		-x		
zyx					z	z
		-y	-x	-x		

Figure 11-10.

Some of the rest of this calculation takes place in the next set of exercises.

Exercises.
201. Develop a proof that x can't be chosen at row six, column two. Thus z is chosen there.
202. Develop a proof that since z is chosen in row six, column two, x can't be chosen in row five, column two. [Hint: Your proof must involve credibility of counterthreats.] Thus z is chosen.
203. Develop a proof that since z is chosen in row five, column two, x can't be chosen in row five, column one. [Same hint.] Thus z is chosen.

Since Exercise 203 tells us z is chosen in row five, column one where z is #2's worst alternative, strategy-proofness by counterthreats entails the appearance of z all along the fifth row. Finally then, z's must appear all along the sixth row or #1 will manipulate from there to row five where no retaliation is possible. Thus we have obtained the rule determined by #1's dictatorship. Exercise 200 tells us that a z in the upper right corner would force the rule determined by #2's dictatorship. Thus with three alternatives and two individuals with strong orders there does not exist a social choice rule satisfying all of

1) the new domain constraint;
2) the range condition;
3) resoluteness;
4) non-dictatorship; and
5) strategy-proofness by counterthreats.

Does there exist a simple generalization to many alternatives, many individuals and weak orders in the same way that the Gibbard-Satterthwaite theorem generalizes the calculations of the last chapter? No one knows. But we will conclude with some exercises touching on these questions. Exercises 204 to 208 deal with generalizing by increasing the number of alternatives to four but staying with two individuals and strong orders. Exercises 209 to 212 deal with generalizing by increasing the number of individuals to three but staying with three alternatives and strong orders.

Exercises.

204. Figure 11-11 shows a social choice rule for two individuals and four alternatives constructed by the following two-step process at each profile: At the first step, #1 selects his most preferred from among {x, y, z}; at the second step, #2 chooses between this first stage winner and w. Show that this rule is not strategy-proof by counter-threats.

	w x y z	w x z y	w y x z	w y z x	w z x y	w z y x	x w y z	x w z y	x y w z	x y z w	x z w y	x z y w	y w x z	y w z x	y x w z	y x z w	y z w x	y z x w	z w x y	z w y x	z x w y	z x y w	z y w x	z y x w
wxyz	w	w	w	w	w	w	x	x	x	x	x	x	w	w	x	x	w	x	w	w	x	x	w	x
wxzy	w	w	w	w	w	w	x	x	x	x	x	x	w	w	x	x	w	x	w	w	x	x	w	x
wyxz	w	w	w	w	w	w	w	w	y	y	w	y	y	y	y	y	y	y	w	w	w	y	y	y
wyzx	w	w	w	w	w	w	w	w	y	y	w	y	y	y	y	y	y	y	w	w	w	y	y	y
wzxy	w	w	w	w	w	w	w	w	w	z	z	z	w	w	w	z	z	z	z	z	z	z	z	z
wzyx	w	w	w	w	w	w	w	w	w	z	z	z	w	w	w	z	z	z	z	z	z	z	z	z
xwyz	w	w	w	w	w	w	x	x	x	x	x	x	w	w	x	x	w	x	w	w	x	x	w	x
xwzy	w	w	w	w	w	w	x	x	x	x	x	x	w	w	x	x	w	x	w	w	x	x	w	x
xywz	w	w	w	w	w	w	x	x	x	x	x	x	w	w	x	x	w	x	w	w	x	x	w	x
xyzw	w	w	w	w	w	w	x	x	x	x	x	x	w	w	x	x	w	x	w	w	x	x	w	x
xzwy	w	w	w	w	w	w	x	x	x	x	x	x	w	w	x	x	w	x	w	w	x	x	w	x
xzyw	w	w	w	w	w	w	x	x	x	x	x	x	w	w	x	x	w	x	w	w	x	x	w	x
ywxz	w	w	w	w	w	w	w	w	y	y	w	y	y	y	y	y	y	y	w	w	w	y	y	y
ywzx	w	w	w	w	w	w	w	w	y	y	w	y	y	y	y	y	y	y	w	w	w	y	y	y
yxwz	w	w	w	w	w	w	w	w	y	y	w	y	y	y	y	y	y	y	w	w	w	y	y	y
yxzw	w	w	w	w	w	w	w	w	y	y	w	y	y	y	y	y	y	y	w	w	w	y	y	y
yzwx	w	w	w	w	w	w	w	w	y	y	w	y	y	y	y	y	y	y	w	w	w	y	y	y
yzxw	w	w	w	w	w	w	w	w	y	y	w	y	y	y	y	y	y	y	w	w	w	y	y	y
zwxy	w	w	w	w	w	w	w	w	w	z	z	z	w	w	w	z	z	z	z	z	z	z	z	z
zwyx	w	w	w	w	w	w	w	w	w	z	z	z	w	w	w	z	z	z	z	z	z	z	z	z
zxwy	w	w	w	w	w	w	w	w	w	z	z	z	w	w	w	z	z	z	z	z	z	z	z	z
zxyw	w	w	w	w	w	w	w	w	w	z	z	z	w	w	w	z	z	z	z	z	z	z	z	z
zywx	w	w	w	w	w	w	w	w	w	z	z	z	w	w	w	z	z	z	z	z	z	z	z	z
zyxw	w	w	w	w	w	w	w	w	w	z	z	z	w	w	w	z	z	z	z	z	z	z	z	z

Figure 11-11.

205. Construct a similar table for the following two-step process: At step one a simple majority vote is taken between x and y and another vote is taken between w and z. The second step is a simple majority vote comparison between the two first step winners. In each case, ties are broken alphabetically. Show that this rule is not strategy-proof by counterthreats.

206. Construct a similar table for the process which works like the one in Exercise 205 except that ties are broken by #1. Show that this rule is not strategy-proof by counterthreats.

207. Construct a similar table for the process that selects the alternative determined by the Copeland calculations; ties broken alphabetically. Show that this rule is not strategy-proof by counterthreats.

208. Spend half an hour modifying these tables trying (unsuccessfully) to construct a resolute, nondictatorial rule satisfying the new domain constraint, the range condition and strategy-proofness by counterthreats.

209. Figure 11 – 12 represents a social choice rule for three individuals and three alternatives. In this table, the preference order of #1 is given down the left side, the order of #2 is given across the top, while the order of #3 is given within each box.

Consider the profile

$$1: zxy;$$
$$2: zxy;$$
$$3: yxz$$

(see the circle).

a. Show that at this profile the rule is manipulable by individual #3.
b. Show that there is no possible counterthreat by #1 alone or #2 alone.
c. Show that there *is* a credible counterthreat by #1 and #2 together.
d. Is the rule strategy-proof by counterthreats?

210. Change the circled x to y. Now is the rule strategy-proof by counterthreats?

211. Construct a similar table for the process that selects the alternative with lowest global Borda count (ties broken inverse alphabetically, i.e., z beats x or y in a tie and y beats x in a tie). Is this rule strategy-proof by counterthreats?

212. Spend half an hour modifying these tables trying (unsuccessfully) to construct a resolute, nondictatorial rule satisfying the new domain constraint, the range condition and strategy-proofness by counterthreats.

	x y z	x z y	y x z	y z x	z x y	z y x
xyz	xyz:x	xyz:x	xyz:x	xyz:x	xyz:x	xyz:x
	xzy:x	xzy:x	xzy:x	xzy:x	xzy:x	xzy:x
	yxz:x	yxz:x	yxz:x	yxz:x	yxz:x	yxz:x
	yzx:x	yzx:x	yzx:x	yzx:x	yzx:x	yzx:x
	zxy:x	zxy:x	zxy:x	zxy:x	zxy:x	zxy:x
	zyx:x	zyx:x	zyx:x	zyx:x	zyx:x	zyx:x
xzy	xyz:x	xyz:x	xyz:x	xyz:x	xyz:x	xyz:x
	xzy:x	xzy:x	xzy:x	xzy:x	xzy:x	xzy:x
	yxz:x	yxz:x	yxz:x	yxz:x	yxz:x	yxz:x
	yzx:x	yzx:x	yzx:x	yzx:x	yzx:x	yzx:x
	zxy:x	zxy:x	zxy:x	zxy:x	zxy:x	zxy:x
	zyx:x	zyx:x	zyx:x	zyx:x	zyx:x	zyx:x
yxz	xyz:x	xyz:x	xyz:x	xyz:x	xyz:x	xyz:x
	xzy:x	xzy:x	xzy:x	xzy:x	xzy:x	xzy:x
	yxz:x	yxz:x	yxz:y	yxz:y	yxz:x	yxz:y
	yzx:x	yzx:x	yzx:y	yzx:y	yzx:x	yzx:y
	zxy:x	zxy:x	zxy:x	zxy:x	zxy:x	zxy:x
	zyx:x	zyx:x	zyx:y	zyx:y	zyx:x	zyx:y
yzx	xyz:x	xyz:x	xyz:x	xyz:x	xyz:x	xyz:x
	xzy:x	xzy:x	xzy:x	xzy:x	xzy:x	xzy:x
	yxz:x	yxz:x	yxz:y	yxz:y	yxz:y	yxz:y
	yzx:x	yzx:x	yzx:y	yzx:y	yzx:y	yzx:y
	zxy:x	zxy:x	zxy:x	zxy:x	zxy:x	zxy:x
	zyx:x	zyx:x	zyx:y	zyx:y	zyx:y	zyx:y
zxy	xyz:x	xyz:x	xyz:x	xyz:x	xyz:x	xyz:x
	xzy:x	xzy:x	xzy:x	xzy:x	xzy:x	xzy:x
	yxz:x	yxz:x	yxz:x	yxz:y	yxz:Ⓧ	yxz:y
	yzx:x	yzx:x	yzx:x	yzx:y	yzx:y	yzx:y
	zxy:x	zxy:x	zxy:x	zxy:x	zxy:z	zxy:z
	zyx:x	zyx:x	zyx:x	zyx:y	zyx:z	zyx:z
zyx	xyz:x	xyz:x	xyz:x	xyz:x	xyz:x	xyz:x
	xzy:x	xzy:x	xzy:x	xzy:x	xzy:x	xzy:x
	yxz:x	yxz:x	yxz:y	yxz:y	yxz:y	yxz:y
	yzx:x	yzx:x	yzx:y	yzx:y	yzx:y	yzx:z
	zxy:x	zxy:x	zxy:x	zxy:x	zxy:z	zxy:z
	zyx:x	zyx:x	zyx:y	zyx:y	zyx:z	zyx:z

Figure 11–12.

Further Reading

Pattanaik's *Strategy and Group Choice* has a good chapter on counterthreats.

Chapter 12. Approval Voting

The second response to the Gibbard-Satterthwaite theorem we consider is to become resigned to the fact that our social choice rules will all have *some* occurrences of manipulability and so direct our search for rules that have *few* such occurrences.

For this to make sense, we must first agree on how to count manipulability occurrences and then show that different social choice rules may yield differing answers to the counting process. Let's start in the three alternative, two person strong order framework. The measure we will take for counting is the number of profiles (boxes) at which the rule is manipulable by at least one individual. It is important to see that a profile is only counted once even if two individuals can manipulate there.

Let's take this measure back to two examples treated back in Chapter 10. In Figure 12-1 is the rule that gives the alphabetically

	x y z	x z y	y x z	y z x	z x y	z y x
xyz	x	x	x	x	x	x
xzy	x	x	x	x	x	x
yxz	x	x	y	y	ⓧ	y
yzx	x	x	y	y	ⓨ	y
zxy	x	x	ⓧ	ⓨ	z	z
zyx	x	x	y	y	z	z

Figure 12-1.

134

earliest of the Pareto optimal alternatives. This rule is manipulable at just four profiles, those with the circles around the alternatives chosen. By way of contrast, Figure 12-2 shows the rule that gives the alphabetically earliest of the alternatives with the lowest global Borda count. Fourteen boxes contain circles to

	x y z	x z y	y x z	y z x	z x y	z y x
xyz	x	x	(x)	(y)	x	(x)
xzy	x	x	x	(x)	(x)	(z)
yxz	(x)	x	y	y	x	y
yzx	(y)	(x)	y	y	z	(y)
zxy	x	(x)	x	z	z	z
zyx	(x)	(z)	y	(y)	z	z

Figure 12-2.

	x y z	x z y	y x z	y z x	z x y	z y x
xyz	x	x	x	x	x	x
xzy	x	x	x	x	x	x
yxz	y	y	y	y	y	y
yzx	y	y	y	y	y	y
zxy	z	z	z	z	z	z
zyx	z	z	z	y	z	z

Figure 12-3.

indicate that the rule is manipulable there. When a colleague pointed out to Borda how easily his procedure could be manipulated by sophisticated voters, Borda retorted with some vexation: "My scheme is only intended for honest men!"

Since societies of "honest men" may be hard to find, we look for low manipulability occurrences among resolute rules satisfying the new domain constraint and where all three alternatives occur in the range. Is the Pareto rule the least manipulable? Is the Borda rule the worst? Try the next problem set.

Exercises.
213. Figure 12–3 shows a modification of a dictatorial rule.

Show that this rule is manipulable at just *three* profiles.
214. Figure 12–4 shows another rule. Show that it is

	x y z	x z y	y x z	y z x	z x y	z y x
xyz	x	x	y	y	x	y
xzy	x	x	y	y	z	z
yxz	y	y	y	y	y	y
yzx	y	y	y	y	y	y
zxy	x	z	y	y	z	z
zyx	y	z	y	y	z	z

Figure 12–4.

manipulable at just *two* profiles.
215. Do there exist rules manipulable at just one profile? (Hard)
216. Figure 12–5 shows the rule which always selects #2's worst. Show this rule is manipulable at *every* profile.

	x y z	x z y	y x z	y z x	z x y	z y x
xyz	z	y	z	x	y	x
xzy	z	y	z	x	y	x
yxz	z	y	z	x	y	x
yzx	z	y	z	x	y	x
zxy	z	y	z	x	y	x
zyx	z	y	z	x	y	x

Figure 12–5.

217. Suppose we avoid rules like the one in Exercise 216 by insisting that the rule pick out an alternative when it is at the top of everyone's ordering. What is then a most manipulable rule? Figure 12-6 shows the rule that obeys our new constraint but otherwise

	x y z	x z y	y x z	y z x	z x y	z y x
xyz	x	x	z	x	y	x
xzy	x	x	z	x	y	x
yxz	z	y	y	y	y	x
yzx	z	y	y	y	y	x
zxy	z	y	z	x	z	z
zyx	z	y	z	x	z	z

Figure 12–6.

picks out #2's worst. Show that this is manipulable at 24 profiles. Show this rule violates the Pareto condition.

218. Suppose we insist further that the Pareto condition be satisfied. What then is a most manipulable rule? Look at Figure 12-7; show that this rule satisfies the Pareto condition but is still manipulable at 24 profiles.

	x y z	x z y	y x z	y z x	z x y	z y x
xyz	x	x	y	x	x	z
xzy	x	x	y	z	x	x
yxz	x	y	y	y	z	y
yzx	x	z	y	y	y	z
zxy	z	x	x	y	z	z
zyx	y	x	z	y	z	z

Figure 12-7.

Though the results of these exercises are suggestive of what can be found at the extremes of manipulabilty, they are narrowly based on our assumptions of two individuals with strong orders and just three alternatives. I don't know of any similar determination of the range of degree of manipulability when we allow more individuals, more alternatives or weak as well as strong preferences.

The questions we have been addressing are part of a design problem. Given certain other constraints on a social choice rule, how far can we go in reducing manipulability? One procedure designed to reduce manipulability but also constrained to do well with respect to other criteria is *approval voting*. Unfortunately, we can't give careful definition to this rule until we can introduce a number of related new ideas. But roughly, everyone submits an unranked list of the alternatives of which they approve and the rule selects the alternatives appearing on most lists.

One advantage to studying approval voting is that it will make us more flexible in thinking about the information input to social choice procedures. Until now we have only examined procedures that admit, as input, profiles of complete preference orderings, one preference ordering for each individual. That is, each individual submits fully ranked information. In this chapter we will also examine so-called "unranked" procedures in which each individual submits an unranked set of alternatives, usually less than all of X. The only (implicit) ranking is that the alternatives in this set are approved and better than the remaining alternatives in X, which are not given approval. So *unranked voting systems* will have profiles of sets as inputs and sets chosen from X (the sole admissible agenda) as output. The set submitted by an individual will be thought of as the set of alternatives for which he casts a vote.

Actually, there is more overlap than there might at first

	{x}	{y}	{z}	{xy}	{xz}	{yz}	{xyz}
{x}	{x}	{xy}	{xz}	{x}	{x}	{xyz}	{x}
{y}	{xy}	{y}	{yz}	{y}	{xyz}	{y}	{y}
{z}	{xz}	{yz}	{z}	{xyz}	{z}	{z}	{z}
{xy}	{x}	{y}	{xyz}	{xy}	{x}	{y}	{xy}
{xz}	{z}	{xyz}	{z}	{x}	{xz}	{z}	{xz}
{yz}	{xyz}	{y}	{z}	{y}	{z}	{yz}	{yz}
{xyz}	{x}	{y}	{z}	{xy}	{xz}	{yz}	{xyz}

Figure 12-8.

seem to be between unranked voting systems and social choice rules; some social choice rules, for example, may receive full preference orderings but will actually ignore almost all that information and really work only with each individual's top-most indifference set.

An unranked voting system is illustrated for the two individual, three alternative case in Figure 12-8. Another unranked voting system in this context appears in Figure 12-9.

	{x}	{y}	{z}
{x}	{x}	{xy}	{z}
{y}	{xy}	{y}	{z}
{z}	{z}	{z}	{z}

Figure 12-9.

This system is presented to emphasize that restriction may be placed on the number of alternatives for which an individual may cast a vote. For the rule in Figure 12-8, the only restriction is that you must vote for at least one; for the rule in Figure 12-9, you can vote only for exactly one. To further examine unranked voting systems we must explore individuals' decisions about what sets to submit to the system. It is assumed that these decisions are based on individual's preferences. The system sees sets, not preferences, but it is preferences that determine *which* sets the systems sees. Among the many possible connections between preferences and submitted sets, we should first emphasize cases called *sincere*. A voter is sincere in his submission if it never happens that he votes for an alternative he considers worse than one he doesn't vote for. Suppose with preference ordering R_i he submits set S. For a sincere submission we have for all x and y

$$(x \in S \text{ and } yP_ix) \text{ implies } y \in S.$$

Thus, with three alternatives and preference ordering

$$i: x(yz)$$

we note $\{x\}$ is not the only sincere submission; $\{x, y\}$, $\{x, z\}$ and $\{x, y, z\}$ are also sincere. But neither $\{y\}$ nor $\{y, z\}$ is sincere. We want unranked voting systems that induce sincere submissions for the same reasons we wanted social choice rules that induce truthful revelation of preferences.

Exercises.

219. What are the seven sincere submissions with ordering (xy)(zw)r?
220. What are the five sincere submissions with ordering xyzwr?
221. How many different sincere submissions are there for an individual with a strong ordering on n alternatives?
222. How many different sincere submissions are there for an individual who is indifferent among all n alternatives?

Of course, a system may not permit an individual to carry out all his sincere submissions. For the individual i above, there were four sincere submissions, and each is allowed by the rule in Figure 12-8, but the rule in Figure 12-9 would only accept $\{x\}$ as a sincere strategy.

To design unranked voting systems that induce sincere submissions, we must explore more deeply what decisions individuals will make about submissions. Or rather, what we really do is discuss what decisions individuals will clearly *not* make. Look now at the unranked voting system partly illustrated in Figure 12-10. Individual #1, whose possible submissions are listed down on the left is now assumed to have strong preference ordering

$$1: xyz.$$

Think about #1 with this ordering trying to choose between submission $\{x, y\}$ and submission $\{x, z\}$. What result is yielded up by this voting system depends not only on #1's decision but also on the submission by #2. *However*, there is still a calculation that #1 can make: no matter what #2 submits, the corresponding outcome

140

	{x}	{y}	{z}	{xy}	{xz}	{yz}	{xyz}
{x}							
{y}							
{z}							
{xy}	x	y	z	x	x	y	x
{xz}	x	y	z	y	z	y	x
{yz}							
{xyz}	x	x	z	y	x	y	x

Figure 12-10.

from 1's submitting $\{x, y\}$ is at least as good (from #1's perspective) as the outcome from his submitting $\{x, z\}$. Further, for at least one submission by #2, the outcome from #1's submitting $\{x, y\}$ is strictly better than the outcome from $\{x, z\}$. For at #2's submission of $\{x, y\}$, #1's submission of $\{x, y\}$ gives $\{x\}$ which #1 strictly prefers to the $\{y\}$ outcome that results if #1 submits $\{x, z\}$. Because both these conditions are satisfied, we say that for individual #1, submission $\{x, y\}$ *dominates* $\{x, z\}$.

Exercises.
223. Show that for 1: xyz and the system of Figure 12-10, $\{x, y, z\}$ also dominates $\{x, z\}$ for #1 but that neither $\{x, y\}$ nor $\{x, y, z\}$ dominates the other for #1.
224. For the system of Figure 12-10 and 2: yxz, can you say anything about domination relationships between $\{y\}$ and $\{x, z\}$?
[Notice it is #2's decision you are considering now.]

The guiding principle of the rest of this chapter is: for a given system and individual ordering R_i, a set S will *not* be submitted by i if there is a set T permitted by the system such that T dominates S for i.

But to exploit this guiding principle fully we must expand somewhat our idea of domination. Look again at Figure 12-8, suppose #1 has ordering 1: (xy)z, and consider whether or not $\{x, y\}$ dominates $\{x, z\}$ for #1. We run into problems rights away. Suppose #2 submits $\{x, y, z\}$. Then if #1 submits $\{x, y\}$ the outcome is $\{x, y\}$; if #1 submits $\{x, z\}$ the outcome is $\{x, z\}$. To find dominance, we need to determine #1's preferences between these *sets*. This didn't arise in establishing dominance (or its absence) in Figure 12-10 because its easy to understand preferences on singleton sets. So easy that back in Chapter 10 we took this way out and only studied resolute rules. But here, where sets are the inputs, sets are the natural outcomes and we try a different route. What we will do is take an individual's *complete* preferences on alternatives and extend these to *incomplete* or partial preferences on sets. For example, with 1: xyz, it seems natural to say not only that #1 prefers {x} to {y} but also that #1 prefers {x, y} to {z}. #1's preferences on x, y and z induce, in a natural way, preferences on some sets made up of x, y and z. But while there are natural induced preferences between *some* sets, that isn't true between *all* sets. From 1: xyz, there is no unique natural extension induced between {x, z} and {y}. Now there is not general agreement on exactly what induced preferences qualify as natural, but the literature on approval voting (which *does* have set outcomes) usually assumes the following three rules where R is an ordering with P the corresponding strict relation:

I. If aPb, then {a}P{b}; if aIb, {a}I{b};
II. If aPb, then {a}P{a, b} and {a, b}P{b};
III. Suppose aRb for all a $\in$ A and b $\in$ B; bRc for all b $\in$ B and c $\in$ C; and aRc for all a $\in$ A and c $\in$ C, where neither A $\cup$ B nor B $\cup$ C is empty; then (A $\cup$ B)R(B $\cup$ C).

It is also assumed that the extended preference ordering over sets satisfies transitivity and such additional consistency conditions as

$$(SP_iT \text{ and } TR_iU) \text{ imply } SP_iU;$$
$$(SR_iT \text{ and } TP_iU) \text{ imply } SP_iU.$$

Exercises.

225. Suppose we have ordering xyz. Show rules I, II and III imply

$$\{x\}P\{x, y\}P\{y\}P\{y, z\}P\{z\},$$
$$\{x\}R\{x, y, z\}, \{x, y, z\}R\{z\}.$$

226. Show these rules do not suffice to order {x, y, z} and {y} by R.
227. What set preferences are determined by (xy)z? [Note: from II we get {y, z}P{z} and from III we get {x, y}R{y, z}, so our consistency assumptions yield {x, y}P{z}.]
228. Show that if S is not empty, SR$_i$S for all i.

Let's take the results of Exercise 227 and return to Figure 12-8 where we were comparing {x, y} and {x, z} for #1 with 1: (xy)z. When #2 submits {x, y, z}, the results are {x, y} if #1 submits {x, y} and {x, z} if #1 submits {x, z}. Now, from III, {x, y}R$_1${x}; from II, {x}P$_1${x, z}; consistency then implies {x, y}P$_1${x, z}. Putting all this together, #1's submission of {x, z} does *not* dominate his submission {x, y}. (We can't say more until we check #1's evaluation of the outcomes at other submissions by #2; see Exercise 229.)

Exercises.

229. Show for the system in Figure 12-8 and 1: (xy)z, that submission {x, y} dominates submission {x, z} for #1.

230. Show for the system of Figure 12-8 and 1: (xy)z that neither {x} nor {x, y} dominates the other. [Hint: Be careful. Although you can show {x, y, z}R{x, z} and you *can't* show {x, z}R{x, y, z}, that combination doesn't mean {x, y, z}P{x, z}.]

231. Show for the system in Figure 12-8 and 1: (xy)z, no submission dominates {x, y} for #1, no submission dominates {x}, no submission dominates {y} and no submission dominates {x, y, z}.

232. In the same framework as Exercise 231, show that every other submission *is* dominated for #1.

Exercises 231 and 232 reveal very strong information about the rule in Figure 12-8 when #1 has 1: (xy)z. Namely, the undominated submissions are precisely the sincere submissions. We have no basis for knowing which undominated strategy #1 would choose, but if we accept the guiding principle, #1 will not choose an undominated submission. So the system of Figure 12-8 is designed so that if #1 has 1: (xy)z, he is induced to make a sincere submission. This is what we are striving for: a system that induces sincere submissions from all individuals at each member of a large class of profiles of preferences.

The unranked voting system of *approval voting* is defined as follows: First, all non-empty subsets of X are permitted; one such subset, S_i, is submitted by each individual, i. Then, the system chooses the set S of all those alternatives x such that, for all y, the number of S_i in which x appears is at least as large as the number in which y appears.

Exercises.

233. Confirm that for two individuals and three alternatives, Figure 12-8 illustrates the approval voting system.

234. Along the idea of the way Figure 11-12 extends the two individual figures of Chapter 11, construct a three individual figure of the approval voting system.

Exercise 233 with our earlier work tells us that approval voting has the desirable property that, at least when he has preference ordering (xy)z, #1 is induced to make a sincere submission. To generalize this, let us say an individual i with preference ordering R_i has *dichotomous* preferences if there are exactly two indifference sets. It has been proven that approval voting always induces sincere submissions when preferences are dichotomous. In fact, it is the only unranked voting system with this property. This is the sense in which approval voting meets our design specifications of minimizing strategic misrepresentation.

Exercise.

235. Check that the rule in Figure 12-8 induces sincere submissions for all dichotomous preferences. [The efficient problem solver will do few cases and let symmetry considerations confirm the rest.]

Approval voting does, of course, have important limitations. In fact, it will have much in common with the social choice rule that we called plurality voting and picked out the alternatives that occurred in the greatest number of top-most indifference sets. In particular, it must sometimes fail to select a Condorcet winner even when everyone votes sincerely. Consider the preference profile

$$1: \text{xyz}$$
$$2: \text{xyz}$$
$$3: \text{yzx}$$
$$4: \text{zyx}$$
$$5: \text{zyx}.$$

Here, y is the unique Condorcet winner. But if everyone adopts their sincere submission of their top-most indifference set, approval voting yields {x, z}. The Condorcet winner is the *only* alternative not chosen! It can be shown, however, that approval voting rejects Condorcet winners less often than most unranked voting systems.

Further Reading

The recommendation here is easy: *Approval Voting* by Steven J. Brams and Peter C. Fishburn (Boston: Birkhuser, 1983). This short paperback contains a wealth of information not only about theoretical properties of approval voting but also about empirical evidence drawn from those organizations that have adopted the system. Included also are "semi-empirical" studies about how certain elections, like recent Presidential races, would have turned out if approval voting had been used.

Chapter 13. Mistakes

In this last chapter, we take up a quite different topic. One desirable property of a social choice rule is that it not be overly sensitive to mistakes. For mistakes are certain to occur. Wishing to honestly record your true preference ordering, you may write it down incorrectly, pull the wrong lever or type in the wrong symbol. The machine may electronically erroneously transpose alternatives in your ordering or incorrectly add up a Borda count. Since this will sometimes happen, you want to design around it. You want to design a rule that is not so sensitive that the outcome will be *drastically* altered by *small* mistakes.

We are involved here in a bit of fine tuning. Early in this book, when we first talked about majority voting, we indicated that *some* sensitivity, or "responsiveness" to individual's preferences was desirable. But now we are saying we want that responsiveness to respect a sense of proportion. While large changes in many preference orderings ought to generate large changes in outcomes, small changes by few – which might be small mistakes – ought to cause small changes in outcomes. This is our protection against errors.

The traditional way of expressing the idea that small changes in inputs generates only small changes in outcomes is *continuity*. Consider for the moment simple mathematical functions that operate on single real number arguments and yield real numbers as outcomes. Take a nice example like $f(x) = 2x + 1$ (see Figure 13–1a). At point x_o, this function yields outcome $2x_o + 1$. If we make a small mistake and use input $x_o + \delta$, the outcome is $2(x_o + \delta) + 1$. The outcome error resulting from the input mistake is

$$[2(x_o + \delta) + 1] - [2x_o + 1] = 2\delta.$$

This output error, 2δ, can be made arbitrarily small by making sufficiently small input mistakes. If you want the output error to be less than .01, that will be the case if the input mistake is less than .005. Small changes cause small results.

Contrast all this with the properties of the following function:

$$g(x) = \begin{cases} 2x + 1 \text{ if } x \leq 3 \\ 2x + 3 \text{ if } x > 3 \end{cases}$$

(see Figure 13–1b).

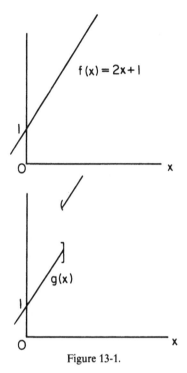

Figure 13-1.

$g(3) = (2 \cdot 3) + 1 = 7$. If we make a mistake and use input $3 + \delta$, with $\delta > 0$, $g(3 + \delta) = 2(3 + \delta) + 3$. The error resulting from the mistake is

$$[2(3 + \delta) + 3] - [(2 \cdot 3) + 1] = 2\delta + 2.$$

This output error can be made smaller by making the input mistake δ smaller, but this time there is a bound on how much we can reduce the output error. At $x = 3$, positive input mistakes, no matter how small, will cause an output error of more than 2. The output error can *not* be made as small as we please just by ensuring that input mistakes are small.

Mathematically, the distinction is that the function f is continuous while g is not. If we want a social choice rule that takes profile u to choice function C_u to be designed to have the property that small input mistakes cause small output errors, we want C_u to be a continuous function of u. To express this more precisely, we will need a suitable concept of nearness: we want to say that when u' is near u (because only a small mistake in recording or processing preferences has been made), then $C_{u'}$ is near C_u (so that output errors are small). At the moment we have no formal idea of when one profile, u', is near another, u, or when one choice function, $C_{u'}$, is near another, C_u. Both of these problems will be settled by getting an idea of what it means for one *ordering*, R', to be near another, R. That will immediately settle the matter for profiles; profile $u' = (R_1', R_2', \ldots, R_n')$ will be near profile $u = (R_1, R_2, \ldots, R_n)$ just when each R_i' ordering is near the corresponding R_i. For choice functions, we can make things work out if we confine our attention only to those rules that have transitive explanations. For then if R' explains C' and R explains C, we will say C' is near C just when R' is near R.

To get a concept of nearness between orderings, we will define a *distance* function, $d(R, R')$, on pairs of orderings.[1] Then R' is near R when the distance between them, $d(R, R')$ is small. We have some freedom in selecting a function to be a distance, but if it is going to correspond to our intuitions, it must satisfy at least the following:

1) $d(R, R') \geq 0$;
2) $d(R, R') = 0$ if and only if $R = R'$;
3) $d(R, R') = d(R', R)$;
4) $d(R, R'') \leq d(R, R') + d(R', R'')$.

This last requirement is a way of saying that by the "distance" between R and R' we mean "shortest distance" and so the shortest distance from R to R'' certainly can't be longer than the particular route that takes the shortest distance from R to R' and then the shortest distance from R' to R''.

Suppose for the moment that we confine our attention to strong orders and a finite number of alternatives. Suppose, for example, we have four alternatives and examine the orderings

$$P: xyzw \text{ and } P': xwyz.$$

Notice that we can get from P to P' by a sequence of transpositions of adjacent alternatives. Starting from P, i.e.,

$$xyzw,$$

first transpose z and w to get

$$xywz;$$

then transpose y and w to get

$$xwyz,$$

i.e., P'. Two transpositions suffice and at least two are necessary; just try all single transpositions on P and see that you never get P'. Of course, more than two transpositions could be used:

$$
\begin{aligned}
P &= xyzw \\
& yxzw \\
& yxwz \\
& ywxz \\
& wyxz \\
& wxyz \\
& xwyz = P'.
\end{aligned}
$$

But two is the smallest number that will suffice. Define $d(P, P')$ to be the smallest number of transpositions that will suffice to change P to P'.

---

[1] This distance function, and its extension later in this chapter, is due to John G. Kemeny; see his "Mathematics Without Numbers," *Daedalus, 88,* No. 4 (Fall, 1959), pp. 577–591.

Exercises.
236. Show that this function satisfies properties 1) to 4) required of a distance function.
237. Compute the distances
    a. between xyzw and wxzy;
    b. between xyzw and wzyx.
238. What is the maximum distance between two strong orders on three alternatives? on four alternatives? on m alternatives?
239. How many orderings are a distance exactly 1 from xyzw?

Next, define the distance between two profiles of preferences to be the *largest* distance between corresponding pairs of preferences: if $u = (R_1, R_2, ..., R_n)$ and $u' = (R_1', R_2', ..., R_n')$, then $d(u, u') = Max\{d(R_1, R_1'), d(R_2, R_2'), ..., d(R_n, R_n')\}$.

Exercises.
240. Show that this function satisfies properties 1) to 4) required of a distance function.
241. Compute the distance between

$$1: xyz$$
$$2: xyz$$
$$3: xyz$$

and the voter paradox profile

$$1: xyz$$
$$2: yzx$$
$$3: zxy.$$

242. What is the maximum distance between two profiles of strong orders on four alternatives?
243. How many profiles are a distance exactly 1 from

$$1: xyzw$$
$$2: ywxz$$
$$3: zywx.$$

However, something more must be done. Even when we restrict our attention to domains of strong preferences, the choice rule C_u may give ties; C_u may only be explainable by orderings that have ties, that have non-trivial indifference, by orderings that are weak, not strong. We could either build in a tie-breaking system so that explanations are always strong and the distance function we already have will apply, or we could extend our concept of distance to cover weak orders as well as strong. This second route would not only allow us to deal with more rules defined on all profiles of strong orders, but also allow us to deal with rules defined on larger domains of weak orders as well.

To make our extension seem more natural, let's go back a step and reinterpret the distance function we already have. Look again at the two orderings P: xyzw and P': xwyz that we have seen are a distance 2 apart. Examine all (unordered) pairs of distinct alternatives: {x, y}, {x, z}, {x, w}, {y, z}, {y, w}, {z, w}. On some of these pairs, the two orderings agree; both, for example, prefer x to y. To each pair on which the two orderings agree, assign the value 0; to each pair, like {z, w} here, on which the orderings are opposite, assign the value 1. Here 1 would be assigned to {y, w} as well as {z, w}. Add up all the assignment values to get 2, the distance between the orderings. This calculation will always yield the distance since each transposition will add a new assignment of 1 to get added in.

Now suppose we have orderings R: xyz and R': x(yz). The pairs are: {x, y}, {x, z} and {y, z}. On the first two pairs, the orderings agree and we would assign 0 to them. On the pair {y, z}, R has y strictly preferred to x and R' shows indifference. Since this is a case intermediate between agreement and opposition, we assign a value intermediate between 0 and 1, namely ½. Adding up for this example yields $d(R, R') = ½$. More generally, the distance between two orderings will be the sum of the assignments of numbers to each pair of distinct alternatives, where 0 is assigned to a pair on which the two orderings agree; 1 is assigned to each pair on which they display opposite strict preference; ½ is assigned to a pair on which one has strict preference and the other is indifferent.

Exercises.
244. Show that this function satisfies properties 1) to 4) required of a distance function.
245. Calculate the distance
   a) between xyzw and (xy)(zw);
   b) between x(yz)(wr) and w(xr)zy.
246. What is the maximum distance between two orderings on three alternatives?
247. How many orderings are at a distance exactly ½ from xyz?

With this extension in hand, we will still define the distance between two profiles to be the maximum distance between corresponding orderings. The distance between two choice functions satisfying transitive explanation will be the distance between the two explanatory orderings.

Given this, what can we say about the possibility of excessive responsiveness of C_u to u? Can we make $C_{u'}$ near to C_u by making u' near to *but different from* u? Of course we can. Consider a constant social choice rule that assigns to all profiles the same explicable choice function. We will have $d(C_{u'}, C_u) = 0$ even when u' isn't near u. Another example is provided by the rule that assigns to $u = (R_1, R_2, ..., R_n)$ the choice function explainable by R_2.

Exercises.
248. Show that for this R_2-based rule we can make $d(C_u, C_u) \leq \frac{1}{2}$ by *any* choice of u' such that $d(u', u) = \frac{1}{2}$.
249. Consider the rule that assigns to $u = (R_1, R_2, ..., R_n)$ the choice function explicable by R_2^*, the opposite of R_2:

$$xR_2^*y \text{ if and only if } yR_2x.$$

Show that for this rule we can make $d(C_{u'}, C_u) \leq \frac{1}{2}$ by *any* choice of u' such that $d(u', u) = \frac{1}{2}$.

But the constant rules and rules based on R_i or its opposite have large drawbacks: they either violate anonymity or the Pareto condition or both. Can we find a social choice rule satisfying the standard domain constraint, the Pareto condition and anonymity such that for all u, $d(C_u, C_u) \leq \frac{1}{2}$ for all u' ≠ u with $d(u', u) \leq \frac{1}{2}$? Let's try some. Consider the global Borda rule at a voting paradox profile

$$u: \quad \begin{array}{l} 1: xyz \\ 2: yzx \\ 3: zxy \end{array}$$

and look at the profile

$$u': \quad \begin{array}{l} 1: (xy)z \\ 2: yzx \\ 3: zxy. \end{array}$$

At u, the global Borda counts of x, y and z are all 6; C_u is explainable by (xyz). At u', which satisfies $d(u', u) = \frac{1}{2}$, the global Borda counts of x, y and z are 6, 5, and 5 respectively; $C_{u'}$ is explainable by (yz)x. $d((xyz), (yz)x) = 1$. So we *can't* ensure $d(C_{u'}, C_u) \leq \frac{1}{2}$ by *every* choice of u' ≠ u satisfying $d(u', u) = \frac{1}{2}$.

Let's try another, a kind of global Copeland rule. Assign to each alternative x the number of alternatives y ≠ x such that on simple majority vote x beats or ties y. Order alternatives by assigned numbers and choose according to this order. Looking at the same two profiles u and u' above, with $d(u', u) = \frac{1}{2}$, we see that at u, each alternative is assigned 2 and the order is (xyz). At u', x, y, z are assigned 1, 2, 1 respectively and the order is y(xz). $d((xyz), y(xz)) = 1$. So again we can't ensure $d(C_{u'}, C_u) \leq \frac{1}{2}$ by every choice of u' ≠ u satisfying $d(u, u) = \frac{1}{2}$.

Exercises.
250. The existence of a distance function between orderings suggests a new technique for designing a social choice rule.[2] Intuitively, we look at a profile $u = (R_1, R_2, ..., R_n)$ and associate with it the ordering R which is, on average, "nearest" the R_i's. Then, from agenda v, pick the alternatives highest in the R ordering. With three alternatives, show that the average distance from 1: abc, 2: a(bc) and 3: bac is less for R: abc than for any other ordering.

[2] See Kemeny, op. cit.

251. One difficulty with the rule of the previous exercise is that more than one ordering may have minimum average distance from the R_i's. Show that there are three distinct orderings that have minimum average distance from the voting paradox profile

> 1: abc
> 2: bca
> 3: cab.

252. Because of the non-uniqueness discovered in Exercise 251, we must patch up our proposed rule. At profile $u = (R_1, R_2, ..., R_n)$, let $S(u)$ be the set of all orderings R that minimize average distance from the R_i's. Then, at agenda v, put into $C_u(v)$ any alternatives that are highest in v for at least one of the orderings in $S(u)$. Show that at the profile of Exercise 251 this rule would have $C_u(\{a, b, c\}) = \{a, b, c\}$.

253. Determine which of Arrow's conditions are satisfied by the rule of Exercise 252.

The distance functions we have worked with only make sense when there are finitely many alternatives. When X is a continuum, as in the pure distribution problem or spatial problems of Chapter 4, defining suitable distance functions is much more difficult and subtle. In exciting recent work, Graciela Chichilnisky has analyzed appropriate distance functions and shown a new impossibility result: there doesn't exist a continuous social choice rule satisfying both anonymity and the Pareto condition.

Further Reading

The Chichilnisky theorem can be found in "Social Aggregation Rules and Continuity, " *Quarterly Journal of Economics* (May, 1982) pp. 337–352.

Mathematical Appendix

I. Sets

Sets are the most frequently encountered objects in this book: sets of individuals, sets of alternatives and social choice rules (which, as functions, are sets) are our main ingredients. A set is an aggregate of its members and can be presented in several ways. Small sets might be presented by enclosing the list of members in brackets:

$$\{x, y, z\} \text{ or } \{1, 2\}.$$

Larger sets might follow this pattern but use dots, "...", to indicate omitted members in the listing:

$$\{1, 2, ..., 16, 17\}$$

or even
$$\{1, 2, ..., n-1, n\}.$$

Larger or more complicated sets may be presented by means of descriptions:

$$\{x \ / \ x \text{ is an integer and } 0 < x < 18\}$$

is read "the set of all x such that x is an integer strictly between 0 and 18." Thus the slash, $/$, in a set description is read "such that."

Membership in a set is indicated by $\in$:

$$x \in \{x, y, z\}, \ 10 \in \{x \ / \ x \text{ is an integer and } 0 < x < 18\}.$$

To say something is not a member of a set we use $\in$ with a slash through it, (remember how a slash changes equality, $=$, to inequality, $\neq$).

$$5 \notin \{1, 2\} \text{ and } (5/2) \notin \{x \ / \ x \text{ is an integer and } 0 < x < 18\}$$

Two sets are *equal* just when they have the same members (order and repetitions in the presentations of sets are irrelevant):

$$\{1, 2\}=\{2, 1\}=\{1, 1, 2\} \text{ and}$$
$$\{x \ / \ x \text{ is an integer and } 0 < x < 18\}=\{1, 2, ..., 17\}.$$

So given two sets, A and B, we write $A=B$ just when, for all x, $x \in A$ if and only if $x \in B$. A set with exactly one member is called a *singleton*. A frequently encountered set is an *empty* set, ø, which contains no members. If B is any set with no members, then ø and B contain the same members (none!) and so by our definition $B=ø$. Thus ø is the *unique* empty set. Any other set is called *non-empty*.

One set, A, is a *subset* of another set, B, just when every member of the first is also a member of the second:

$$\text{for all } x, x \in A \text{ implies } x \in B.$$

We then write $A \subset B$.

$$\{1, 2\} \subset \{1, 2, 3\} \text{ and}$$
$$\{1, 2\} \subset \{x \: / \: x \text{ is an integer and } 0 < x < 18\}.$$

To say A is *not* a subset of B, then, is to say A contains some member that is not also in B. Clearly that can't be said if A is the empty set, so the empty set is a subset of B no matter what B is! Now $A \subset B$ has been defined in such a way that it is possible A and B are equal. In fact, $A = B$ just when both $A \subset B$ and $B \subset A$. When we want to say $A \subset B$ but $A \neq B$, we say A is a *proper subset* of B.

Next we consider three ways of making new sets from given sets. The first way is to take two sets, A and B, and construct the new set that consists of the members of A that are also members of B. The result is called the *intersection* of A and B and is written $A \cap B$. Thus $x \in A \cap B$ if and only is $x \in A$ and $x \in B$.

$$\{1, 2, 3, 4\} \cap \{3, 4, 6, 9\} = \{3, 4\}$$
$$\{1, 2\} \cap \{1, 2, \ldots, 17\} = \{1, 2\}$$
$$\{1, 2\} \cap \{x, y, z\} = \emptyset.$$

The intersection operation satisfies several rules: for all A, B and C,

$$A \cap A = A$$
$$A \cap B = B \cap A$$
$$A \cap (B \cap C) = (A \cap B) \cap C$$
$$A \cap \emptyset = \emptyset.$$

Intersection is also closely related to our subset concept: for all A, B,

$$A \subset B \text{ if and only if } A \cap B = A.$$

The second construction starts with two sets, A and B, and combines them in the *union* of A and B, the set of all things that are members of A or members of B or both. We write $A \cup B$.

$$\{1, 2, 3, 4\} \cup \{3, 4, 6, 9\} = \{1, 2, 3, 4, 6, 9\}$$
$$\{1, 2\} \cup \{1, 2, \ldots, 17\} = \{1, 2, \ldots, 17\}$$
$$\{1, 2\} \cup \{x, y, z\} = \{1, 2, x, y, z\}.$$

To express rules satisfied by union, we again let A, B and C be any three sets. Then:

$$A \cup A = A$$
$$A \cup B = B \cup A$$
$$A \cup (B \cup C) = (A \cup B) \cup C$$
$$A \cup \emptyset = A.$$

Union is also closely related to subsets: for all A, B,

$$A \subset B \text{ if and only if } A \cup B = B.$$

It also intersects with the union operator:

$$A \cap (B \cup C) = (A \cap B) \cup (A \cap C).$$
$$A \cap B \quad A \cup B.$$

Our final construction again starts with two sets A and B and builds the *complement* of B in A, the set of all members of A that are not in B. This is written A-B.

$$\{1, 2, ..., 17\} - \{1, 2\} = \{3, 4, ..., 17\}$$
$$\{1, 2\} - \{1, 2, ..., 17\} = \emptyset$$
$$\{x, y, z\} - \{1, 2\} = \{x, y, z\}.$$

For all sets A, B, we have

$$A - \emptyset = A$$
$$A - A = \emptyset$$
$$A = (A\text{-}B) \cup (A \cap B).$$

Again we have a connection with the subset idea:

$$A \subset B \text{ if and only if } A\text{-}B = \emptyset.$$

Complement interacts with both union and intersection:

$$A - (B \cup C) = (A\text{-}B) \cap (A\text{-}C)$$
$$A - (B \cap C) = (A\text{-}B) \cup (A\text{-}C);$$

the complement of the union is the intersection of the complements and the complement of the intersection is the union of the complements.

Many important sets are built out of *ordered lists*. A list is presented in parentheses: $(x_1, x_2, ..., x_n)$ is a list of *length* n. Lists have the crucial property that they are equal just when they are of the same length and the elements in corresponding positions are equal:

$$(x_1, x_2, ..., x_n) = (y_1, y_2, ..., y_n)$$

just when

$$x_1 = y_1 \text{ and } x_2 = y_2 \text{ and } ... \text{ and } x_n = y_n.$$

Thus

$$\{1, 2\} = \{2, 1\} \text{ (as sets) but } (1, 2) \neq (2, 1) \text{ (as lists)}.$$

Lists of length two, or *ordered pairs*, are especially important as they are used to define functions. As an intermediate step, we define relations. Given sets A and B, a *relation* from A to B is a set R of ordered pairs having the special property that the first element of each ordered pair is a member of A while the second element of each ordered pair is a member of B. Here are some relations from $\{x, y, z\}$ to $\{1, 2\}$:

1. $\{(x, 1), (y, 2)\}$
2. $\{(x, 1), (y, 1), (z, 1)\}$
3. $\{(x, 1), (x, 2)\}$
4. $\{(x, 2)\}$
5. $\emptyset$.

If A and B are both the set of all people, living or dead, and R is the relation "is the father of", we have

$$(\text{John Neville Keynes, John Maynard Keynes}) \in R.$$

As this example suggests, we often alter our notation a little and write xRy rather than (x, y) ∈ R.

Among the relations from A to B are some important special cases called functions. A relation f from A to B is a *function* from A to B just when

a) Every member of A is the first element of some ordered pair in f, i.e., if x ∈ A, there is at least one y ∈ B such that (x, y) ∈ f.; and
b) No member of A is the first element of two distinct ordered pairs in f, i.e., if x ∈ A, then (x, y) ∈ f and (x, z) ∈ f imply y=z.

A function f from A to B associates with each member x of A exactly one element y of B with (x, y) ∈ f. When f is a function from A to B, we write f: A→B and then if (x, y) ∈ f we write f: x→y or y=f(x). The word *mapping* is also used as a synonym for function. Of the five relations from {x, y, z} to {1, 2} listed above, only the second is a function from {x, y, z} to {1, 2}. The others all fail to use z as first element of an ordered pair; the third also fails because it assigns two different B values to x. The one function,

$$\{(x, 1), (y, 1), (z, 1)\}$$

is a *constant* function; it assigns the same B value to every A member.

The relation "is a father of" also fails to be a function, both because some people have fathered no one and because some people have fathered more than one. However, the relation "has, as father, " is a function.

If f is a function from A to B, the *domain* of f is A; it is the set of all first elements of ordered pairs in f. The set of all second elements is called the *range* of f and is a subset of B. The range of the function {(x, 1), (y, 1), (z, 1)} is just {1}. (Notice that {1} is not the same thing as 1.)

Among the functions, one special class is the *permutations*. Given a set A, a function f: A→A is a permutation on A if two conditions are satisfied:

i) No member of A is the second element of two distinct ordered pairs in F;
ii) The range of f is A, i.e., every member of A is the second element of some ordered pair in f.

If f is a permutation on A, then every member of A occurs exactly once as a first element and exactly once as a second element. Both conditions are needed; suppose Z is the set of all integers (positive, negative and zero). Then f: Z→Z defined by f: x→2x satisfies ii) but not i); it is a function, but not a permutation. Also, g: Z→Z defined by

$$g: z \to \begin{cases} z+1 \text{ if } z \geq 0; \\ z-1 \text{ if } z < 0. \end{cases}$$

is a function but not a permutation [here i) is satisfied, but ii) isn't since 0 is not in the range of g]. h: Z→Z given by

$$h: z \to z+1$$

is a permutation as is the function j on {x, y, z} given by

$$x \to y, \ y \to z \text{ and } z \to x.$$

II. Logic and Proofs.

Given two statements, p and q, we say "p implies q" whenever p is false or q is true or both. That is, "p implies q" is true unless p is true and q is false. We also say "if p, then q" or "p is a sufficient condition for q" or "q is a necessary condition for p." For example, A ⊂ B means: for all x,

$$\text{if } x \in A, \text{ then } x \in B.$$

Accordingly, ø ⊂ B is true because x ∈ ø is false.

We write "p if and only if q" to mean p and q satisfy both p implies q *and* q implies p. Thus, "p if and only if q" is true just when both p and q are true or both p and q are false.

There are about a half dozen proofs in this text and you are asked in the Exercises to provide many more. If proofs make you uncomfortable, you might read Daniel Solow's *How to Read and Do Proofs* (New York: Wiley, 1982). Here we will describe two proof techniques that will be useful.

The first technique is called *proof by contradiction.* Suppose we want to prove p implies q. A *direct* proof would start by assuming p and then deriving q; but this may be very hard. Remembering that p implies q can fail only when p is true and q is false, we may try to show that this combination of p true and q false can not happen. To do this, we start by assuming both that p is true and q is false and then deriving something that is clearly false, like 1=2 or some other "contradiction."

The second technique is proof by *mathematical induction.* Suppose we have a statement about n, where n can be any positive integer. Examples:

1. There is an integer larger than n;
2. n is the square of another integer;
3. The sum of the first n positive integers is ½n(n+1).

Some sentences like these are true for *all* positive integer values of n; others, like #2 here, are not true for all positive integers (though they may be true for some). For statements that are true for all positive integers, we clearly can not provide separate proofs for each integer; there are too many. So we do it slightly differently, by proving two things

a) (The *Basis Step*) First we prove the special case n=1. (This is usually trivially easy.)
b) (The *Induction Step*) Next we show that *if* the statement is true when n=k, *then* it must also be true when n=k+1.

Thus, having shown the statement true for n=1 in the Basis Step, an application of the Induction Step shows the statement is true for n=2. Another application of the Induction Step then shows the statement is true for n=3, and so on.

Look at Example #1 above: There is an integer larger than n.
Basis Step: When n=1, this is easy, e.g., 7 is larger than 1.
Induction Step: Suppose the statement is true for n=k, that is, there is an integer, say m, larger than k:

$$m > k.$$

Adding 1 to both sides gives

$$m+1 > k+1.$$

But since $m+1$ is an integer, this says there is an integer larger than $k+1$; we have shown the statement is true for $n=k+1$ assuming it is true for $n=k$.

For another illustration, look at Example #3:

$$1+2+\ldots+(n-1)+n=\tfrac{1}{2}n(n+1). \tag{1}$$

Basis Step: When $n=1$, both the left hand side and right hand side of (1) are 1.
Induction Step: Assume (1) is true for $n=k$, i.e.,

$$1+2+\ldots+(k-1)+k=\tfrac{1}{2}k(k+1). \tag{2}$$

We wish to establish the truth of (1) when $n=k+1$, i.e., using (2) we wish to prove

$$1+2+\ldots+(k-1)+k+(k+1)=\tfrac{1}{2}(k+1)(k+2). \tag{3}$$

But look at the left hand side of (3):

$$1+2+\ldots+(k-1)+k+(k+1)=\tfrac{1}{2}k(k+1)+(k+1)$$

using (2). So the left hand side equals

$$\tfrac{1}{2}k(k+1)+(k+1)=(k+1)(\tfrac{1}{2}k+1)$$
$$= (k+1)(\tfrac{1}{2}k+\tfrac{1}{2}\cdot 2)$$
$$= (k+1)\tfrac{1}{2}(k+2),$$

which clearly equals the rights hand side of (3). This is what we wanted: (1) with $n=k$ implies (1) with $n=k+1$.

Fittingly, our last remark about proofs notes the symbol ■ which appears as a marker at the end of a proof.

Answers and Hints to Selected Exercises

4. $N_{+1}(D) > n/2$ implies $N_{-1}(D) < n/2$ so implies $N_{+1}(D) > N_{-1}(D)$. Similarly, $N_{-1}(D) > n/2$ implies $N_{-1}(D) > N_{+1}(D)$.

6. f is not defined for example at $(0, 0, \ldots, 0)$.

7. This rule does satisfy universal domain.

8. Suppose for k, $1 \leq k \leq n$, there is no i with $k = s(i)$. Then s maps $\{1, 2, \ldots, n\}$ to $\{1, 2, \ldots, k-1, k+1, \ldots, n\}$ so there must be some element in $\{1, 2, \ldots, k-1, k+1, \ldots, n\}$ that is the image under s of two different elements of $\{1, 2, \ldots, n\}$. This is a violation of the one-to-one assumption.

9. d and d are permutations via the identity map $s: i \rightarrow i$.

10. If d and d' are permutations via the map s, then d' and d are permutations via the inverse map s^{-1} defined by $s^{-1}(j) = i$ just when $j = s(i)$.

11. If d and d' are permutations via map s and d' and d'' are permutations via map t, then d and d'' are permutations via the *composite* map $t \circ s$ defined by

$$t \circ s(i) = t(s(i)).$$

13. Satisfies anonymity.

14. Violates anonymity.

16. Violates neutrality.

17. Satisfies neutrality.

18. When $D = D'$.

19. Suppose $i \neq j$. Then $d_j'' = d_j'$ and $d_j' = d_j$, so $d_j'' = d_j$.

22. For absolute majority rule,
$f(0, 0, \ldots, 0) = 0$ and $f(+1, 0, \ldots, 0) = 0$
showing a violation of positive responsiveness.

23. Violates positive responsiveness.

24. Violates positive responsiveness.

25. No. f might be -1 at every list except $(+1, +1, \ldots, +1)$ where f assigns 0.

28. See Kenneth O. May, "A Note on the Complete Independence of the Conditions of Simple Majority Decision," *Econometrica*, 21 (Jan., 1953), pp. 172–173.

36. $26 \cdot 25$.

37. $9 \cdot 10$.

38. $26 \cdot 26 \cdot 26$

39. $26 \cdot 25 \cdot 24$.

40. $9 \cdot 10 \cdot 10$.

41. $\frac{1}{2}(52 \cdot 51)$.

42. $(52 \cdot 51 \cdot 50 \cdot 49 \cdot 48)/(5 \cdot 4 \cdot 3 \cdot 2 \cdot 1)$

43. Hint: Since there are more alternatives than individuals, some alternative must be a the top of at least two individual's preference orderings.

44. No. If it did satisfy single-peakedness, so would the voting paradox profile (erase 1:xyz).

45. No. If it did satisfy single-peakedness, so would the voting paradox profile (erase w).

48. Yes.

49. Yes.

50. No.

59. Because $M > 0$.

60. $z_i + \sum_{j \neq i} z_j = M$.

and each $z_j \geq 0$

65. a to 0 to 10 to x_1 to b; b to a.

67. Draw contours through x_1; no three overlap.

70. No.

71. Yes.

75. If x is a Condorcet winner, $n(x) = N - 1$ so $n(x) \geq n(y)$ for all y and x will be chosen under the Copeland Rule.

76. With two alternatives, x and y,

$$n(x) = \begin{cases} 1 \text{ if } N(xP_iy) \geq N(yP_ix) \\ 0 \text{ otherwise} \end{cases}$$

$$n(y) = \begin{cases} 1 \text{ if } N(yP_ix) \geq N(xP_iy) \\ 0 \text{ otherwise.} \end{cases}$$

So $n(x) \geq n(y)$ and is chosen under the Condorcet Rule just when $N(xP_iy) \geq N(yP_ix)$, i.e., when x is chosen under simple majority vote.

77. If y beats z, then so does x; $n(x) \geq n(y)$. But x beats y and y doesn't beat x. Hence $n(x) > n(y)$ and so y doesn't maximize n.

79. y can't be in *any* top-most indifference set.

82. See the situation in Exercise 83.

85. Use mathematical induction.

89. Use mathematical induction.

91. xyz zyx z(xy)

 xzy x(yz) (xy)z

 yxz (yz)x (xyz)

 yzx y(xz)

 zxy (xz)y.

93. Use the fundamental counting rule.

94. 4^3, n^3.

95. 3^{13}.

96. C may select any of the $2^4 - 1$ non-empty subsets of X.

97. C must be defined at one agenda of size four, where 15 subsets may be cho-

sen and at four agendas of size three at each of which $2^3-1=7$ subsets may be chosen. Apply the fundamental counting rule.

98. Along the lines of the answer to 97, there are now also six agendas of size two from each of which $2^2-1=3$ subsets may be chosen.

103 a. $C(\{x, y\})$ $= \{x, y\}$ $C(\{x, z\})$ $= \{x, z\}$ $C(\{x, w\}) = \{x\}$
$C(\{y, z\})$ $= \{y\}$ $C(\{y, w\})$ $= \{y, w\}$ $C(\{z, w\}) = \{z, w\}$
$C(\{x, y, z\})$ $= \{x, y\}$ $C(\{x, y, w\}) = \{x, y\}$
$C(\{x, z, w\})$ $= \{x, z\}$ $C(\{y, z, w\}) = \{y, w\}$
$C(\{x, y, z, w\}) = \{x, y\}$

106. No one can force inclusion of higher indexed alternatives when lower indexed alternatives are available.

111. No. Consider a profile where everyone in S is indifferent between x and y while everyone in the complement S'-S strictly prefers x to y.

113. No.

116. No.

119. N is the only decisive set.

128. Only N is decisive for x_1 against x_0; any set one smaller than N is decisive for x_0 against x_1.

129. Only N is decisive.

130. No. No.

136. $C_u(\{x, y\}) = \{x, y\}$; $C_{u'}(\{x, y\}) = \{x\}$.

144. See the example in Exercise 115.

145. Consider the Ω defined by
aΩb, bΩb, cΩc, aΩb, bΩa, bΩc, cΩb, aΩc.

157. Let $X = \{x, y\}$ and $C_u(\{x, y\}) = \{x, y\}$ unless $N(xP_iy) = 1 \le N(yP_ix)$ (with $C_u(\{x, y\}) = \{y\}$ or $N(yP_ix) = 1 \le N(xP_iy)$ (with $C_u(\{x, y\}) = \{x\}$. Then N-{i} is locally but not globally decisive.

160. a. $C(\{x, y, z\}) = \{x, y, z\}$
b. All except independence of irrelevant alternatives.

161. All except having transitive explanations.

166. In Example 2, each individual is decisive for x_1 against x_2 but no coalition is decisive for x_2 against x_1.

169. For violation of the Pareto condition examine profile
1: zxyw
all others: ywzx.

185. You *do* have enough information at both. The rule *is* manipulable at u''; it is *not* manipulable at u'.

187. This rule is manipulable at
1) row three, column five;
2) row four, column five;
3) row five, column three;
4) row five, column four.

188. Let row i, column j be indicated by $<i, j>$. Then the fourteen manipulable profiles are at positions
$<1, 3>$, $<1, 4>$, $<1, 6>$,
$<2, 4>$, $<2, 5>$, $<2, 6>$, $<3, 1>$,
$<4, 1>$, $<4, 2>$, $<4, 6>$, $<5, 2>$,
$<6, 1>$, $<6, 2>$, $<6, 4>$.

192. Consider Exercise 214.

193.

	x y z	x z y	y x z	y z x	z y x
xyz	x	x	y	y	y
xzy	x	x	y	y	z
yxz	y	y	y	y	y
yzx	y	y	y	y	y
zxy	x	x	y	y	z

198. $<6, 4>$. No credible counterthreat to #1's manipulation to $<5, 4>$ since at $<6, 4>$, x is #2's worst also.

202. If there is an x at row six, column two, #1 could manipulate to row three or four where #2 can not retaliate.

203. If there is an x at row five, column two, #1 could manipulate to row six getting z. The only possible counterthreat is to y but since that is also #2's worst, the counterthreat won't be credible.

204. At 1: yzxw, 2: zwyx, #1's worst, w, wins. So 1: zwxy is a manipulation without a counterthreat.

205. See the table on the following page.

209 c. To profile
   1: zyx
   2: zyx
   3: yzx.

d. Manipulation by #2 from
   1: zyx   to 1: zyx
   2: zxy   2: yxz
   3: yzx   3: yzx

has no counterthreat.

213. $<6, 1>$, $<6, 3>$, $<6, 4>$.

214. $<2, 5>$, $<5, 2>$.

214. No.

219. {x}, {y}, {x, y}, {x, y, z}, {x, y, w}, {x, y, z, w}, {x, y, z, w, r}.

220. {x}, {x, y}, {x, y, z}, {x, y, z, w}, {x, y, z, w, r}.

221. n.

222. 2^n.

	w	w	w	w	w	w	x	x	x	x	x	x	y	y	y	y	y	y	z	z	z	z	z	z
	x	x	y	y	z	z	w	w	y	y	z	z	w	w	x	x	z	z	w	w	x	x	y	y
	y	z	x	z	x	y	y	z	w	z	w	y	x	z	w	z	w	x	x	y	w	y	w	x
	z	y	z	x	y	x	z	y	z	w	y	w	z	x	z	w	x	w	y	x	y	w	x	w
wxyz	w	w	w	w	w	w	w	w	w	w	w	w	w	w	w	w	w	w	w	w	w	w	w	w
wxzy	w	w	w	w	w	w	w	w	w	w	w	w	w	w	w	w	w	w	w	w	w	w	w	w
wyxz	w	w	w	w	w	w	w	w	w	w	w	w	w	w	w	w	w	w	w	w	w	w	w	w
wyzx	w	w	w	w	w	w	w	w	w	w	w	w	w	w	w	w	w	w	w	w	w	w	w	w
wzxy	w	w	w	w	w	w	w	w	w	w	w	w	w	w	w	w	w	w	w	w	w	w	w	w
wzyx	w	w	w	w	w	w	w	w	w	w	w	w	w	w	w	w	w	w	w	w	w	w	w	w
xwyz	w	w	w	w	w	w	x	x	x	x	x	x	w	x	x	w	x	w	w	x	x	w	x	w
xwzy	w	w	w	w	w	w	x	x	x	x	x	x	w	x	x	w	x	w	w	x	x	w	x	w
xywz	w	w	w	w	w	w	x	x	x	x	x	x	w	x	x	w	x	w	w	x	x	w	x	w
xyzw	w	w	w	w	w	w	x	x	x	x	x	x	w	x	x	x	x	x	x	x	x	x	x	x
xzwy	w	w	w	w	w	w	x	x	x	x	x	x	w	x	x	x	x	x	x	x	x	x	x	x
xzyw	w	w	w	w	w	w	x	x	x	x	x	x	w	x	x	x	x	x	x	x	x	x	x	x
ywxz	w	w	w	w	w	w	w	w	w	w	w	w	y	y	y	y	y	y	w	w	w	w	y	y
ywzx	w	w	w	w	w	w	w	w	w	w	w	w	y	y	y	y	y	y	w	w	w	w	y	y
yxwz	w	w	w	w	w	w	x	x	x	x	x	x	y	y	y	y	y	y	w	w	x	x	y	y
yxzw	w	w	w	w	w	w	x	x	x	x	x	x	y	y	y	y	y	y	x	y	x	x	y	y
yzwx	w	w	w	w	w	w	w	w	w	x	x	x	y	y	y	y	y	y	z	y	z	z	y	y
yzxw	w	w	w	w	w	w	x	x	x	x	x	x	y	y	y	y	y	y	z	y	z	z	y	y
zwxy	w	w	w	w	w	w	w	w	w	x	x	x	w	w	w	x	z	z	z	z	z	z	z	z
zwyx	w	w	w	w	w	w	w	w	w	x	x	x	w	w	w	y	y	y	z	z	z	z	z	z
zxwy	w	w	w	w	w	w	x	x	x	x	x	x	w	w	x	x	z	z	z	z	z	z	z	z
zxyw	w	w	w	w	w	w	x	x	x	x	x	x	w	w	x	x	z	z	z	z	z	z	z	z
zywx	w	w	w	w	w	w	w	w	w	x	x	x	y	y	y	y	y	y	z	z	z	z	z	z
zyxw	w	w	w	w	w	w	x	x	x	x	x	x	y	y	y	y	y	y	z	z	z	z	z	z

224. $\{x, z\}$ does not dominate $\{y\}$. You don't have enough information to determine if $\{y\}$ dominates $\{x, z\}$.

225. For $\{x\}R\{x, y, z\}$, apply rule III with
$A = \emptyset,\ B = \{x\},\ C = \{y, z\}$.

237. a. 4.
    b. 6.

238. $3,\ 6,\ \tfrac{1}{2}m(m-1)$.

239. Three: yxzw; xzyw; xywz.

241. 2.

242. 6.

243. $4 \cdot 4 \cdot 4 - 1 = 63$.

245. a. 1.
    b. 6½.

246. 3.

247. 2.

Subject Index

Managing Editors:

Wulf Gaertner
Fachbereich Wirtschaftswis-
senschaften, Universität
Osnabrück, Postfach 4469,
4500 Osnabrück, FRG

Jerry S. Kelly
Department of Economics,
Syracuse University, Maxwell
Hall, Syracuse, NY 13210,
USA

Prasanta Pattanaik
Department of Economics,
Faculty of Commerce and
Social Science, The University
of Birmingham, P.O. Box 363,
Birmingham B15 2TT, UK

Maurice Salles (Coordinating
Editor), Institut des Sciences
de la Décision, Université de
Caen, 14032 Caen Cédex,
France

Editors:

K. J. Arrow, S. Barbera,
A. Bergson, C. Blackorby,
J. H. Blau, G. Bordes,
G. Chichilnisky,
J. S. Coleman, P. Dasgupta,
B. Dutta, R. Dworkin,
J. Ferejohn, P. C. Fishburn,
W. V. Gehrlein, L. Gevers,
G. Heal, M. Kaneko,
G. H. Kramer, J.-J. Laffont,
E. S. Maskin, B. Monjardet,
H. Moulin, Y.-K. Ng,
B. Peleg, N. Schofield,
T. Scitovsky, R. Selten,
A. K. Sen, P. Suppes,
K. Suzumura, W. Thom-
son, B. Williams

Springer-Verlag
Berlin Heidelberg New York
London Paris Tokyo

. . . a focal point for collective choice and welfare:

Up to now, contributions to welfare economics and social choice and voting theory have been spread over a large number of journals coming from various disciplines including economics, mathematics, operations research, philosophy, political science, psychology, and sociology. **Social Choice and Welfare** serves as a focal point for issues in collective choice and welfare for these and other disciplines.

Social Choice and Welfare publishes original research, survey papers and book reviews on the ethical and positive aspects of welfare economics and collective theory. The appropriate topics comprise social choice and voting theory (normative, positive and strategic sides) as well as all aspects of welfare theory (Pareto optimality; welfare criteria; fairness, justice, and equity; externalities; public goods; optimal taxation; incentives in public decision making; cost-benefit analysis; etc.). Articles on choice and order theory are also published if their results can be applied to these topics. Papers both verbal and formal in style are considered.

CPSIA information can be obtained
at www.ICGtesting.com
Printed in the USA
LVHW021924171122
733288LV00005B/182

9 783662 099278